Too Young to Remember

Too Young to Remember

Julie Heifetz

Wayne State University Press   Detroit   1989

Library of Congress Cataloging-in-Publication Data

Heifetz, Julie.
  Too young to remember / Julie Heifetz.
    p. cm.

  Bibliography: p.
  ISBN 0-8143-2026-0 (alk. paper).   ISBN 0-8143-2027-9 (pbk. : alk.
paper)
  1. Holocaust survivors—United States—Biography.   2. Holocaust,
Jewish (1939–1945)—Personal narratives.   3. Women, Jewish—United
States—Biography.   4. Jews—United States—Biography.
5. Immigrants—United States—Biography.   I. Title.
E184.J5H533   1989
940.53′15′039240—dc19   88-20898
                                                                                                          CIP

To the women of this book,
for the privilege of entering their lives

Contents

Foreword

Adolf Hitler's Third Reich lasted but twelve years, yet the devastation and changes it wrought in the political and demographic configuration of Europe—with their world-wide ramifications—remain long after its demise. Among the nations and peoples that suffered from the onslaught, all have regained and surpassed their pre-war populations except Jews and Romanis (Gypsies). These two peoples sustained such massive deaths, including the women and children who represented their future potential, that they have not been able to recoup their losses

Numbers alone do not tell the whole story. Anyone who thinks the defeat of Hitler and his regime put an end to the scourge should read this book. For here, in only six autobiographical narratives, we glimpse the extent of the havoc accomplished by the "Final Solution of the Jewish Question." The six children whose stories are related in this book are part of the tiny remnant that survived that catastrophic destruction.

When the Holocaust is mentioned, the usual and immediate association made is to the death camps. Yet anyone who has done any reading on the subject knows that this was only one component of Hitler's "Final Solution." Jewish experiences varied enormously, depending on all sorts of factors. Particularly important was the country where Jews lived when the Nazis gained power in or over that country and the speed with which the annihilation program was put into practice in that country. Therefore, it is not surprising to find that the two women in this book who were children in Germany when Hitler came to power did not experience ghettos, labor or death camps because their families were able to leave Germany before the war began. (This, however, does not mean that the girls did not suffer from the Nazi regime.) Nor is it surprising that all three of the women who were children in Poland remember the ghettos the Germans set up soon after they defeated and occupied that country, and that two of these women spent some time in various camps including Auschwitz (while the third spent years pretending to be a Polish Christian). Hitler's war on Jewish children demonstrates the racial-biological premises on which the Nazis operated, for every Jewish child was automatically deemed unworthy of life merely by being born of Jewish parents or grandparents. According to Nazi theory, nothing could alter their evil heritage.

The ever-changing circumstances and multiple traumas endured by each family is shown by the fact that even though there are only six personal accounts, we are told about labor camps, concentration camps, the ghetto-transit camp of Terezin, the death camp of Auschwitz including its infamous medical experiments, a child camp, a *Lebensborn* camp, and finally the DP (Displaced Persons) camps set up after the war by the Allied powers.

While this book gives us important information about what it was like to be a Jewish child in Nazi Europe, it is not only, or primarily, a collection of Holocaust memoirs. What we have is a more unusual and, for that very reason, valuable work: stories that begin just prior to Hitler's impact on the lives of these families and continue into the present. Six women recall the Nazis' anti-Jewish war as they experienced it at a very young age, and as they saw or felt it affect their parents and other adults around them. Even with such a small sample, we learn about some of the less frequently mentioned experiences of Jews during this time.

Lebensborn, for example, may be unknown to some readers. The name refers to the so-called positive aspects of the Nazi racial program: appropriately selected "Aryan" women were impregnated by supreme "Aryan" males (members of the SS) in order to create Hitler's master race, and non-German Gentile children were tested and measured to find those with sufficient "Aryan" characteristics to make them suitable for inclusion in Germany's society. These children were forcibly taken from their families for this purpose. The children who did not meet the standards of the Nazi "racial scientists" were considered to be disposable matter and were treated accordingly, usually by being sent to a murder camp.

The reader who has read or heard many survivor accounts will not be too surprised—though no less appalled—at any of these revelations. But these accounts do not stop with the end of the war and supposed liberation as so many do. We learn about the continuing difficulties and traumas these young girls experienced, even those fortunate enough to have been able to remain with parents throughout the terrible years or to rejoin one or both of them afterwards.

The post-war months saw the struggle to survive continuing in different forms: the dangers of illegal flight across borders (made necessary by new threats to Jewish life in Poland), the hardships of weeks of travel in open cattle cars, endless lines of stunned people in the DP camps, repeated disappointment over efforts to leave Europe, post-war illness and breakdown of parents as well as the children's own health problems. Survivors endured loss over and over again: a new friend would suddenly leave for Australia, Canada, South Africa, or the United States; a cousin or friend who could not cope with the loneliness or hopelessness would commit suicide; an only surviving cousin would succumb to tuberculosis acquired during the years of malnutrition. Jewish families felt the loss of family, friends, and community even more keenly outside the DP camps for they were surrounded by a Gentile, Christian population from which most Jews had been "culled" by the Nazis and their helpers. Jewish teenagers found themselves markedly isolated by being only one or two among many hundreds of others their age. The problems of normal adolescence were augmented by this demographic abnormality and the fears their childhood experiences had imposed.

However, there was light as well as darkness during these months. In the DP camps, children were free to run and play (even though parents were often obsessively protective and restrictive), to be with other children among whom they were no longer the only one who was "different," to be able to go to school and learn and have something to think about besides death, to acquire friends from all over Europe as well as a multiplicity of languages "as if by osmosis," and to discover that there could be fun in life.

Often the problems and fears the youngsters had were a reflection of, or a reaction to, the difficulties and fears the adults were experiencing also. Although frequently they could not understand everything that was happening, the children became better at coping with the rapidly changing situations than their parents. Of course, coping often meant repressing frightening memories or pretending things were better than they were.

Readers may be most disturbed to learn of the extreme unhappiness and loneliness of survivors once they were in the United States. Expectations of happiness were summarily shattered when many of them discovered that "no one wanted any part" of them. Even relatives who had had a hand in helping them immigrate ignored them. Despite the hardships of the DP camps, everyone there had been in the same situation: people knew what their neighbors had suffered over the years and did not expect them to be happy and "normal" immediately, and difficulties with strange languages could be overcome with the help of the multilingual community. In Europe there were many others who had lived through the Nazi nightmare—even if they had not suffered to the same extent; and in England food and housing shortages and other reminders of the war lingered on for years. But in America, survivors (including German Jews who arrived in the late 1930s) were isolated in an unfamiliar culture, with an unknown language, and a people who had not experienced at first hand any of the horrors of National Socialism. They were now isolated from other Jews who had shared their fate, survived, and been met by new problems. While the children learned the language quickly and became their parents' translators, they were doubly isolated by their successful Americanization. They could not identify or be identified by any peers with a similar background, and adult survivors assumed they were "too young to remember" and did not treat them as members of the survivor group. Nor did these adults want to listen to the children's memories, even though they knew how important it was for themselves to be able to talk to someone else about that past. (Psychiatrists and social workers also failed to take these childhood experiences into account when the women later sought help.)

The truly remarkable aspect of these accounts is the strength that is demonstrated by the girls (and the women they became). They could not depend on their parents for help because of the parents' own difficulties; roles were often reversed and mothers and fathers leaned on the youths. Without any professional help, these young women determined to create lives for themselves.

Despite their handicaps, the six women in this book have fought to surmount the exigencies of childhoods distorted by the Nazis' determination to annihilate all European Jews, have fought to prevail over the despair that threatened to become overwhelming, and have fought to establish homes for themselves and their families in which human dignity and perhaps even hope could be sustained.

There is much to be learned from these accounts. They provide details about the Holocaust itself and the post-war struggle of these Jewish families and individuals to rebuild their lives in the shadow of that catastrophe. They show how fearful events and the emotional turmoil such events cause can disorient and shatter people and families in ways that do not end when threatening situations finally cease. Surviving may actually compound the problems with which such people have to live. Many survivors have a sense of guilt for being one of the few to escape death when multitudes, including family members, did not. Moreover, they feel they are carrying a heavy burden of responsibility to live on behalf of all those who perished.

The Holocaust destroyed the usual parent-child relationship—not just at the time, but permanently. These children were made graphically aware of the powerlessness of children, who are at the mercy of others' decisions and without the right even to question them. Ambivalence toward their parents carried over into the post-war years. Parents' efforts to reestablish a home and some security are recognized as herculean struggles, yet this does not eradicate resentment at the changes the Holocaust had caused in a mother or a father or both, and at the demands still made of the child.

Such feelings were, and remain, frightening to acknowledge; they threatened a present and future that were questionable enough in any case. And so they were not acknowledged. Various methods were used to compensate for or bury them. Thus, the full accounts we have here only emerged gradually and painfully as the women talked to Julie Heifetz. Never before had this information been shared with anyone else, and many of the incidents and the feelings associated with them had lain buried for several decades. The women began to achieve an understanding of some of their behavior patterns only as they uncovered the hidden memories. Their experience demonstrates the error in advising people to forget such unhappy events. The past and its threat can be dealt with only when it is brought out of the deep recesses into consciousness. This realization is further supported by another assemblage of personal recollections—of French Jews who as children had their father, mother, or both parents deported while they remained behind with other families or in institutions.* There are many parallels between these men and women and Heifetz's women in emotional reactions, compensatory behavior, and general attitudes toward life: blaming parents, feeling guilty, inability to be happy, loneliness, identity problems, and particularly the burying of memories until someone finally persuaded them to talk about the experience.

Julie Heifetz's book also tells us much about the role that neighbors and society play in hindering people from being whole and feeling worthy of consideration. In a way quite unforeseen these six accounts evidence how much traditional social attitudes regarding male-female roles can hamper the achievement of wholeness and fulfillment by women. For these six women such attitudes were almost as serious a problem as the more radical expressions of rejection and hatred they had known, and greatly aggravated their situation. Yet we also find the positive effect that one understanding person can have on the life of an individual. When any of

---

*Claudine Vegh, *I Didn't Say Goodbye;* translated by Ros Schwartz (New York: E. P. Dutton, Inc., 1984).

these women began to be helped, it was as a result of being able to talk to someone—particularly someone outside the family—and being accepted by that person as a human worthy of respect.

We are grateful to Julie Heifetz for helping these women to gain a new perspective on their lives, and for sharing the stories with us so that we may understand more fully the long-term consequences of Hitler's war of annihilation against the Jewish people. We may hope that she will also provide us with accounts of men who were child survivors, to see what similarities and differences may exist in their experiences, their means of adjusting, and to what extent they have succeeded in dealing with their past.

Alice L. Eckardt

Acknowledgments

I would like to express my gratitude to Rabbi Robert Sternberg and the St. Louis Center for Holocaust Studies for their interest in this book, and for helping facilitate my work; to Jill Fisher and Rodney Stucky for their generous listening as the book progressed; to my parents, Rae and Robert Nussbaum, for developing my capacity to listen to others and the desire to write down what I have heard; and to my husband, Gary, and my sons, Steve and Doug, for refueling me at the end of every day.

Introduction

          In the spring of 1986, after a reading of first-person narrative poems I had written based on my interviews with survivors of the Holocaust, a woman introduced herself and asked if she might make an appointment to talk with me—there was something important she wanted to discuss. I sensed that she had more than an objective interest in my work interviewing survivors and writing about their experiences, with which she seemed quite familiar. She was a good deal younger than any of the survivors I had ever met, had no accent, and seemed "fully American." It did not occur to me that she was a survivor, but when we talked, her need to discuss her experiences as a child who had survived the Holocaust was painfully clear. She wished to tell her story and have me seek out and interview other child survivors as well. "I'm sure I'm not the only one," she said hopefully.

          With her help, I began to understand the particular dilemma of child survivors. They are difficult to identify as survivors. Survivors who emigrated to the United States as children assimilated quickly into American life. Hungry to learn, to play, to be thought of as "normal," they dropped their accents and any telltale signs of their early European roots. Older survivors recognized each other immediately when walking down the street though they might have been strangers before, and formed groups and support systems that extend wherever they travel. The child survivor was shuttled off to schools where the rest of the children were unaware of the difficulties in Europe and the particular experiences of the new child, isolated and alone. There were no networks to inform child survivors of other children who had survived, no groups in which they could feel they belonged. According to the Jerome Ryker International Study of Organized Persecution of Children living in Europe and the United States, child survivors living in America feel especially alienated. One woman recalled her attempts to disguise herself from being identified with her Holocaust experiences as "a Riverdale fantasy. That I was just like Veronica in the comic strips with normal parents and a house and dates on Saturday nights, where my biggest worries were what to wear to the Prom." But behind the fantasy lurked the real experiences and the isolation caused by not being able to identify with "regular Americans" or older Holocaust victims.

Of the six million Jewish victims of the Holocaust, perhaps 1.2–1.5 million were children. There are no statistics available as to how many children survived, but the belief that none did has persisted. Even some adult survivors are unaware that children did survive. Only in the past ten years has literature about the Holocaust dealt with children who lived through Nazi persecution in camps, in hiding places, or under disguised identities in communities at large. A child survivor may have grown up thinking that he or she is the only Jewish child to have survived. The problem is not merely one of being identified. There has been little encouragement for child survivors to remember and talk about their experiences during the Holocaust. If parents survived, discussions about those years tend to revolve around the parents' memories, often neglecting the children's experiences. It is understandable that parents would not want to think their children suffered emotionally from those experiences, or to hear they still bear the scars of those times. It would be easier for them to think the children do not remember. Spouses and children of child survivors also have difficulty listening to the painful memories of those early years and encourage child survivors not to think back, not to dwell on the past, to put it away and go on.

Child survivors have been disregarded as reliable sources of information. Researchers have not sought out child survivors, instead interviewing important people, leaders whose perceptions and memories they trust more than those of children. Perhaps they, along with the rest of the world, have been guilty of wanting to deny that such horrors could have been forced onto the young and innocent. Difficult as it has been for the world to listen to adult survivors' stories and enter their pain, it has been even more terrible to think of the sufferings of children during the Holocaust.

Children were routinely among the first to be murdered in Nazi Germany. Hoess, the Auschwitz commandant, explained that children were killed by the Nazis because they could not work and would therefore be a drain on the economy. Himmler stated that children had to be killed or they would eventually avenge the killing of their parents.

In all types of societies and families, children are often treated with disregard—as if they are mindless, second-class citizens, mere extensions of their parents' needs and wishes. Their experiences are ignored or dismissed. Their stories and memories are thought to be unreliable. Their anxieties and sadnesses go unheard, locked in loneliness. This is child abuse—in a nonphysical form. As a result of this treatment, many child survivors are reluctant to identify themselves and tell their stories, thinking they will not be believed. Some child survivors' fantasy lives are rich and fully developed, which adds to their worry that perhaps the episodes they recall were imagined. It is important for these survivors to sort out their fantasies from reality. Psychiatrists have given little help in bringing child survivors' stories to light. More and more oriented toward thinking in terms of organic causes for emotional disturbances, psychiatrists have not provided survivors with the opportunity to think back and gain relief from their past.

Most of those I interviewed who were children during the Holocaust had not talked about their experiences before to anyone—friend, relative, or professional. Many had shied away from participating in Yom Hashoa commemorations and felt out of place with an older generation of survivors. They had been told too often that they could not possibly remember events that happened to them when they were so young. They lived with a special loneliness, continuing to feel discounted and alienated. Initially, they spoke as though their parents and others of the older generation were the real survivors and more important, as though they were not entitled to their own pain and their own lessons from the past. For my purposes, I defined a child survivor as one under the age of thirteen between 1933 and 1945 who lived in Europe, who was an eyewitness to persecution, whose life was threatened directly or indirectly, and whose psychological, emotional, and physical life was altered in an essential way by the Holocaust, both during and after those years.

Initially I interviewed men as well as women. Eventually I decided to write a book that included only the women's stories. I made this decision because of my experiences as a therapist working with mothers of very young children, and because—as a woman—I am especially interested in how these women's experiences as young girls affected their later choices of careers, husbands, child-raising practices, sexuality. In general, "his"tory has been told more often than "her"story, although recently more autobiographical works of women who experienced the Holocaust have been published. Women are willing and able to explain their experiences clearly and authoritatively when they are convinced that people will believe them and can handle what they have to say. It is generally easier for women to tell their stories to female interviewers, whose interviewing style may be less aggressively intrusive, allowing the story to unfold slowly and with sensitivity to the interviewee. The women I interviewed for this book felt more comfortable speaking to a female interviewer, particularly about sexual matters or other experiences unique to women.

Although women in this book were children during the Holocaust whose lives were altered by it in an essential way both during and after the war, there are many differences among them. Their families represent a wide range of educational, socioeconomic, and religious backgrounds and nationalities. Some survived with parents, others alone. Their life-styles, attitudes, and occupations today are equally diverse. All six did marry and have children, but two later divorced. All are Jewishly identified but range in their practices from Orthodoxy to unaffiliated status. Four had never spoken about their experiences until these interviews. Three had sought professional help regarding emotional difficulties, but their counselors had not delved into their experiences during the Holocaust or linked those past traumas with present difficulties. Two contracted life-threatening diseases, and one of them died during the writing of this book. The names of the women, except for Hedy, have been changed to protect their privacy.

I have chosen to present the women's stories in uninterrupted first-person narratives for two reasons. This method, as opposed to the usual ''she said'' style of case studies, allows the reader to maintain an emotional as well as intellectual response, much as I experienced in listening. It is my wish to present the survivor's personality as well as the facts of her existence by keeping the attention on her words, her ''voice print,'' as Dr. Judith Kestenberg calls it, rather than drawing the reader's attention to my voice or interviewing technique. I accomplished this weaving of each tale—maintaining the integrity of the speaker's voice—by beginning with many individual interviews collected over approximately a year's time. With the exception of Frederika's (whom I never met, but whose oral history was sent to me along with a biographical summary of events up to and including her death), the interviews were tape-recorded and transcribed. From the transcription, I reordered the stories in logical time sequence, cutting and pasting as though the speakers had begun at the beginning and had spoken through to the present time without repetition or omission or questions to elicit information. This kind of editing leaves out some aspects of the interviews essential to the process. The reader does not get a sense of the time and trust necessary for the interviewer to unfold the sifting through of confusing or conflicting memories, or the resistance the interviewee may have had to uncovering painful truths. There is some distortion of the speakers' syntax where I have simplified rambling and ungrammatical sentences too confusing for a reader to understand. I have used these survivors' words, and, whenever possible, their sentence structure for their own stories. This way we have a window on each woman's thinking, her educational level, and her unique style. I wanted not to make the interviewees subjects, but to establish a vehicle through which they may speak for themselves, telling their own stories clearly. Once I finished writing a woman's narrative, I made comments that included my own observations, which I discussed with each woman. They needed to feel a sense of collaboration in this process and pride in what they were able to share and contribute about the lives of children who survived the Holocaust.

Readers may be curious about missing dates, conflicting details. Conducting the interviews, I decided it was most important to follow the thread of the survivor's story without constantly checking whether information was factually accurate at all times. Constant questions as to whether events were actual or imagined make an interviewee defensive and interfere with her ability to tell her story freely. What is most important in these accounts is not the external accuracy of details, but how child survivors perceived the truth. Their beliefs about what was happening became an internal reality and the basis for actions at the time and in the future. It is not particularly relevant, for example, to know if a child heard actual bombs after the war, or whether she merely thought she heard them. She continued to experience fear after liberation. Although the war was supposed to be over and she had been returned to "safety," she did not feel safe. In trying to understand the world as she understood it, many times there is a confusing puzzle. The confusion and missing links are more important to child survivors' lives than "the facts" of the Holocaust historians may supply.

The women I interviewed and came to know in the process of writing this book are remarkable. Perhaps only exceptional children could have survived, using their intellect, cooperation, creativity, and personal charisma discerningly to do whatever was required to stay alive. Whatever the unique facts of their past, these women are intelligent, strong individuals, despite scars caused by their experiences during the Holocaust. Or perhaps in part because of them. A psychiatrist who has worked with survivors and their children, Dr. Anna Orenstein, herself a teenage survivor of Auschwitz, decries the often-used term "survivor syndrome" and the emphasis placed on the abnormalities of the survivor population that has caused professionals and others to overlook the personal strengths and contributions of child survivors to society. Deprived of normal childhoods, exposed to persecution, somehow the majority of child survivors have gone on to lead normal lives, proving productive in occupations, often becoming part of the helping professions related to social service.

Of course, there are problems common to child survivors. Many who as children were lucky enough to escape with their lives when millions perished harbor a sense of shame about having been so fortunate. They feel inadequate to live up to the special privilege of having been the "chosen ones." They do not believe that having been saved, they have any right to complain about life's anxieties or worries. Many later blamed themselves for having prevented their parents' escape. They wonder if their mothers and fathers might not have fled Europe while there was still time—before the true horrors began—had they not been saddled with a child. Yet not all child survivors labor under "survivor guilt." Some take special satisfaction in their personal and professional accomplishments, knowing that they have achieved success not for themselves alone, but for all who would have contributed to society had they survived. Instead of guilt over survival, some child survivors recognize their importance as being part of a new generation that will carry on for the family and for the Jewish people.

Child survivors witnessed their parents' helplessness and experienced the loss of parental protectiveness under persecution. Some parents chose to abandon their children; other families were forced to separate. Parents died, or simply disappeared. Since the children did not know they would not be seeing their parents again, they did not have a chance to say goodbye. Because there were no funeral services, no memorial candles, no graves, no known dates of death, children had difficulty realizing their parents had died and could not mourn.

These children had no chance to work through the unfinished business of childhood. They missed the developmental process of weaning themselves slowly away from their parents' thoughts and wishes and grow into their own voices of authority. They did not have an opportunity to form other meaningful relationships while maintaining a loving, supportive one at home or to see their parents through adult eyes. As adults, child survivors tend to idealize parents who did not survive.

It is difficult for many child survivors to recognize and deal with their rage at their parents' inability during those years to function as parents, to shield them from the atrocities. Many question why their parents would have had children at such a time. Four of the women interviewed for this book said they were the result of unplanned pregnancies that their mothers had probably wanted to abort. Whether or not this was true these women live with the fantasy that their parents had never really wanted them, that they were burdens from the start.

Some child survivors find it difficult as adults to allow themselves true emotional intimacy. "You have to depend on yourself in life; there is nobody else. I can't stand the thought of being a burden to someone," a survivor stressed. Her early years convinced her that leaning on someone else was an impossibility. Survival without a mother or father meant learning to live by her own wits, by her own hard work. There was no sense in turning to others for comfort or help. In Auschwitz, those who could not walk alone were left to die. As so many loved ones died, children learned that loving someone meant painful loss.

It is not known how many children committed suicide during the Holocaust, but many who were separated from their parents gave up the fight to continue to live. They did not want to face the horrors alone. Yet some children fought for survival even after they were the only one of their family alive. Perhaps they had a stronger survival instinct or perhaps they had received enough love and nurturing from their parents before the Holocaust to be strengthened by those early experiences. Starving prisoners sometimes consoled themselves by remembering foods their mothers had prepared or particular scenes from home. A survivor of Auschwitz emphasized in her interview that the confidence she gained from knowing she had been loved by her family was a confidence no one could take away from her.

Children whose parents survived with them in ghettos, camps, or hiding did not feel as frightened or depressed as those who lost their parents. The relationships between parents and children who survived together became extremely complicated. Children and parents spent abnormal amounts of time together without privacy or boundaries between generations. Children overheard their parents' conversations, their love-making, their terror. Parents insisted that their children stay close, fearing what might happen if they were separated. Such children never learned to separate from their parents without trauma. Four of the women interviewed for this book referred to themselves as "good little girls" whose survival had depended on being obedient to their parents' instructions about keeping secrets, staying quiet, or telling lies. Although they were too young to understand the reasons behind these instructions, they responded to the urgency for doing what they were told. They learned not to question or demand, but to protect their parents from additional worries that they might create by being too demanding. As adults, these women continued to define themselves in terms of others' expectations, not giving much thought to their own needs.

Adults who as children were not directly subjected to physical violence during the war but would have been victims had they not escaped from Europe share some of the emotional scars of child survivors. Although they would not call themselves survivors of the Holocaust, the atmosphere in Europe from 1933 to 1945 bred confusion and insecurity in Jewish children, even if they escaped the ghettos and camps. If these children were particularly aware of and sensitive to their environment, the anxieties they picked up remained incomprehensible and overwhelming. Children saw and heard a great deal of what happened around them, although parents may have tried to hide the facts and their own feelings. The saying "The walls have ears"—a familiar phrase at the time—reflects the insecurity and distrust people felt about being overheard by the wrong ears that were everywhere. When children do not understand what is happening, they make up their own explanations to fill in the gaps of information. Their fantasies can be as frightening as the realities. Many who, as children, left Europe before 1939 do not consider that later problems with depression, anxiety, or separation stem from psychological traumas created between 1933 and 1939. "Absolutely nothing happened to me," they say, denying any connection with others victims of persecution. Their lives were altered in a permanent and essential way by the Holocaust, yet they do not recognize it as the cause of some of the emotional difficulties that have followed them into adulthood.

Problems for child survivors who had remained in Europe continued long after liberation. Many did not know their true identities. Their names had been changed, birth certificates altered, religions switched, in an attempt to keep children hidden. Some Jewish children were adopted by non-Jewish families; others were placed in Catholic institutions by parents who may or may not have been alive after the war to claim them. Changes in identity often were made when children were too young to remember their true families or religious roots. In 1945 Europe became a sea of separated, dislocated families trying to reconnect. It took many years after the end of the war for these children to sort out the truths of their lives. Some never untangled the complicated facts from fiction.

After the war, many Jewish young women who were child survivors developed romantic relationships with German non-Jewish men or fantasized about doing so. They described a fascination and hatred for German males, identifying with the aggressors while wishing to punish them for the devastation to humanity the Nazis had caused. Some married German non-Jews whose families more than likely had participated in the Nazi cause. Two women whose stories are in this book describe their spouses as having Nazi-like personalities, being abusive to their wives and treating them as inferior beings without rights. Once in the United States, children who earlier had been uprooted by the Holocaust found themselves still rootless. Their families had to move from one house to another, one neighborhood to another, one city or state to another, and the children from one school or grade to another, forcing them to repeatedly be the outsiders, the greenhorns, trying to learn new rules. Emigrants needed people to care about them, to help with the transition. Although agencies and organizations did what they could, the physical and emotional needs of survivors' families were enormous, and not enough adequate help was available. The unspoken rule was to adapt and not complain. The children continued to feel isolated and alienated in an environment where they were not understood and which was different from their pasts. Children often became responsible for helping parents adjust to the new language and customs rather than receiving help themselves. Many women who had been so uprooted repeated this pattern after marrying, moving from city to city, house to house, as their husbands' jobs changed, constantly having to adapt to new environments. There were no periods of mourning over what was left behind, the familiar surroundings, friends, or homes. They were expected to adapt quickly and without complaints. These women continue to feel an absence of any real home. They say, "I don't really have a home anymore. Not since the war. I don't really have a country, either."

Child survivors with siblings born after the war notice differences between themselves and these siblings. Two separate families seem to exist within one family: one triad is the parents and the child of the Holocaust, the other is the parents and the child born after the Holocaust.

For many women who had been children during the Holocaust, having children of their own was extremely important as a return to normalcy, an affirmation of life. While being isolated at home with young children at home is often stressful, for some child survivors motherhood caused extreme anxiety and depression. Those who had been deprived of nurturing and normal childhoods found it difficult to impart a sense of confidence and security to their children. Separation problems resurfaced in their relationships with their children. It is difficult to give to others what has not been received during childhood.

Although scars still remain from the early years of confusion, anxiety, deprivation, and pain, child survivors have continued to grow in their personal lives. As a group, they are a shining example of the capacity of the human spirit to survive even unthinkable horrors. Their presence gives us hope and courage to fight our own battles against inhumanity and oppression of any kind. After hearing a survivor's story, one student said, "I'm not a survivor of the Holocaust, but I was abused as a child myself. I have tried to suicide four times; I have been in and out of mental institutions over the last five years. But if she could hang on for all those years of pain and suffering, I guess I can too. Listening to her makes me want to try."

The women I interviewed for this book were enthusiastic about the interviews, and chapters based on their stories. They experienced a great sense of relief in being able to talk in depth about their experiences after all these years. Many of them came to new understandings as to the effect of those early years on their roles as women, daughters, wives, mothers, or workers. As they reread their stories, they saw they were not dirtied by their experiences. They realized their strengths and what they had been able to make of their lives.

It is true that childhood memories have gaps of information and sometimes confusing perceptions, but this is also true of twenty-year-old memories of older survivors. With time and patience, many of these distortions can be sorted out and understood. It is important for child survivors to have the chance to reexamine those childhood years with an empathic and interested listener who values their past experiences as a part of them. The children hold the truth of their own experiences. They must be allowed to speak, for their sake and for ours. No one else, not parents nor older siblings nor any historian, can describe what they saw, heard, worried about in the dark of those years or in the years that have followed. Child survivors are the ultimate authority about the past and its effects on their lives. We can help them to recall it if we do not get in the way by assuming they were too young to remember.

1
Anna

Anna is an attractive, well-groomed, youthful-looking woman. She immediately impressed me as being bright, articulate, and informed, professional in her bearing. It is not apparent by her age, appearance, or language that she is a survivor of the Holocaust. She gives the impression of being American-born. This impression has helped reinforce her feelings of dislocation from her past and has distanced others from her experiences.

Anna was born in Radom, Poland. Her earliest memories are filled with her parents' anxieties over the future. "I was in a crib and my parents and grandparents were in my room. There was all this fear and chaos. There were trying to regroup." She could smell their fear, and it was a smell that clung to her throughout her childhood. When she was two years old, the town was turned into a forced labor camp. The old and the young were sent away. Anna's parents devised a plan to hide her in a false ceiling in the barracks in which they and other Jewish couples lived. She describes her three years spent in hiding, her liberation and move to Czechslovakia, her year in a DP [displaced persons'] camp, her move to the United States. Through it all, there is a torrent of rage that surges underneath. It was at her request that the interviews for this book were begun.

Anna was reliable and conscientious in the interviewing process. I easily understood how she has been successful in securing an advanced degree in social work and how she uses her skills administering programs for the aged. As we began to work together, Anna reported her story

27

without tears, her face earnest but expressionless, her voice without emotion or hesitation. When I mentioned her great control, she sighed deeply, as though letting go for a moment, and explained that she was trying to be objective and accurate so people would believe her. Until we began our interviews, the Holocaust had been treated as though her parents were the survivors, not she. Yet when she spoke, I could see in her the little girl she once was, locked away quiet and forlorn in an attic. During the most formative years of her life, when a child normally strives for autonomy, she had been told, "Whatever happens, you may not cry. Your life depends on it."

By our last interview, one and half years after we began, Anna had more insight into her behavior and was working at establishing an identity as a single woman. At the end of this interview, I told her I was eager to write her story and give it to her, that I hoped she would be able to see herself in this mirror as I saw her—as a lovely, intelligent, capable woman. It was the only time she cried.

I am forty-five years old, and I'm tired of being discounted, of being told I was too young to remember those years I was hidden away from the Nazis. No one has wanted to listen to me about this; not my parents, and certainly not my ex-husband. He didn't want to know that part of me, that Holocaust part. It's repulsive to him, it's unclean. Even my children don't want to know. They've inherited this attitude, this taboo about my background. I'm beginning to understand how I've contributed to this, how I've discounted my own experiences. But I'm tired of pretending that the Holocaust was not my story, or that I couldn't possibly remember, just because I was two years old when I was hidden away.

I was born in Borislav, in the oil country of Poland. At that time in history, sons had to take their mothers' names, as the government illegalized paternal holdings. My father took his mother's maiden name of Markell, so that was my maiden name. I was born without even the right to my father's family name.

My father was born in Borislav, too. When he was a young man, he left to live in Vienna, to study art. But he was more of a ne'er-do-well than a serious student. He took some art courses, but he played a lot, did a lot of concerts, theater, a lot of womanizing. This is his reputation even today, relatives still talk about his adventures and romances. On Yom Kippur in Vienna, everybody else would fast and go to the synagogue, but he would go to a sidewalk cafe and eat sausages. He was very free, and more than a little rebellious against traditional Judaism. But he came back to Borislav.

My mother had never left. She wasn't even remotely as sophisticated or educated as my father. She was the youngest of eight children, a good Jewish girl, growing up to take care of her parents and her religion, to light the candles on Friday night and observe all the holidays. When my parents got married, the world shook. It was 1940. I mean, the timing of their marriage and their family planning absolutely overwhelms me. I have no idea why they did what they did, whether it was just denial on their part, or whether it was the only way to hold on to their optimism. But they were married in 1940, and I was born in 1941, although by then the writing was very darkly on the wall; they couldn't set up a household of their own, there was no work, people were already being taken away, and it was just a matter of time. I once asked my mother why, why they had me, considering what was happening. She just shrugged her shoulders and said they had to live.

The first memory I have is of my grandmother, my father's mother. I was still in a crib, and she was in the room with me, with a lot of other people bustling around, semihysterical, trying to regroup. I don't know what had happened in that moment, but I could smell their fear, that's what I remember most. Then when I was a year old, the Poles built a ghetto in our town. I have been told that only two children from our town survived, and I am one of them.

When my parents became aware that all of the children were being taken away, they made a plan for hiding me. They built a false ceiling in one of the rooms in the camp, a narrow space where I was kept while my mother and father were sent to forced labor along with the other adults. It was a plan that required a collusion among many people to keep me up there. I'm not sure why I was the one chosen out of all the children, except my mother tells me that even though I was only two years old, I could understand everything that was going on, and I was very good. I was out of diapers by the time I was a year old, and she says I was adorable. I remember that at times I was taken down out of my little space and put on a table, passed around as though I were the child of the town. They brought me whatever extra food was available, so I never got sick. I often think of how they must have resented me, the other adults, when their own children were dead, and there I was alive and well. My mother says I couldn't possibly remember back then, that I was too young, they must just be stories I've heard. But I do remember being passed like a doll from one to the other. My father could speak German from all his years in Vienna, and the Nazis used him as an interpreter. When there was any news, he'd bring it back to the place where we lived, so he was important. Occasionally he'd get things from the Germans. One day he went to work and the German commander's dog had destroyed his prize vegetable garden. The commander was furious and told my father to get rid of the animal. My father brought him back to the ghetto and it may have taken ten seconds before that dog was killed and butchered, every inch of him, including the skin, cooked and eaten.

I have no idea what our building looked like from the outside, because once I went in, I never came out again for the three years until we were liberated. But I remember a window looking out on the buildings in the town; stone buildings, old with flaking paint, and children playing beyond the ghetto wall. There must have been a common kitchen and a bathroom, although I can't remember smells. But stairs, I do remember stairs, narrow stairs. I remember every time anybody came, I was conscious of footsteps as he ran up those stairs. And it was dark and empty in the false ceiling where I was kept, except for some old rags I used to play with. I remember holding them, twisting them, touching their softness like stuffed animals to keep me company all those hours I was alone. As I tell you all of this, I keep thinking someone's going to say it isn't true, that it never happened, some historian with scholarly authority, because I was only a child. But the more I talk, the more layers get peeled away, the more I feel these aren't just stories, this is what happened to me. Even though there are tremendous gaps in my memory, I do remember some things. One day my father came home with poison. He was so excited about it. I heard my mother and father arguing, he wanted to give the poison to me, but my mother wouldn't let him. I remember her crying and begging him. Maybe he wanted to spare me any more suffering, or maybe he wanted to end his own by getting rid of me, I must have been such a worry to him. If I cried, I could have the whole family, the whole town killed for hiding me away like that. I wish I knew how he felt about me then, but I never discussed it with him. I was simply afraid of him after that. I was more afraid of him than the Germans. Even after the war, that poison was a wall between us we never knocked down.

At night I slept in the same bed with my parents. When they got back from work every day, when they knew it was safe, they took me down from my little space. There were so many noises at night; people moaning, coughing, and the sounds of people making love, too, even my parents. My mother got pregnant in that ghetto. She was so undernourished by then it was amazing that she still menstruated and could conceive, but she did. Of course she didn't show very much, the clothes she wore hung off her bones. The night she gave birth I was there near her. Some women helped her while she was in labor, and the baby was born; a boy, my little brother. But my father and some men came to take him away. Maybe they used that poison that had been meant for me, or maybe they just smothered him; but he was born, and they took him away like a piece of garbage. Sometimes I think it would have been easier to have been the one to die. All my life I've lived with being the chosen of the chosen, and it's impossible for me to justify.

One day my mother was sick and stayed home from work. It was late afternoon and she was playing with me on our bed. Suddenly she heard someone coming up the stairs. She shoved me under the bed, into a pile of clothes and rags, and hissed at me to keep quiet. A soldier came into the room with a dog on a leash. I could see his boots from under the bed, and I could hear him questioning my mother. Then the dog stuck his head under the bed. I could see his fangs and smell his breath. He started growling and I screamed, even though I knew I was supposed to be quiet. The officer reached under the bed and pulled me out. "What's this?" he demanded. I don't know what she told him, but whatever she said, he just left. And he never came back or told anyone about me. I don't know why. Maybe he had a child and could understand, or maybe my mother promised him something . . . maybe she gave herself to him. There's always been a lot of that, women using their bodies to pay off men. I only know that for several days she lived in fear waiting for him to turn us in. But he never did . . . he never did. And now that I'm telling you this, I can still feel that dog's breath on my cheek. I've always been afraid of dogs, of German shepherds, but I never knew why until this moment.

Three years I lived this way; hidden. Then suddenly the war ended and we were liberated. Oh, and it felt nice to be outside. I do remember that; the smell of the grass, all the wild flowers. And there was this wall, it couldn't have been very tall, but I was tiny and I couldn't get down. I remember screaming in terror. And I remember running and laughing; being a child for the first time. We moved to a house in the country, with some of my uncles and my aunt. My little cousin Rachel was with them, who was my age. During the war when Rachel was a baby, her father was killed and her mother gave Rachel to a non-Jewish couple who promised to take care of her. By the time the war was over Rachel was four or five years old, and naturally my aunt wanted her back. But that couple was too attached to her to want to give her up. And Rachel didn't know her own mother anymore. There was this terrible fight. I remember them in the street, this couple pulling at this little child from one side, and my aunt pulling at her from the other, ready to tear her in half, and Rachel crying and confused. Rachel was my first friend. We slept in the same bed and we talked a lot. We told each other our dreams. I remember one dream I told her of standing at a door watching someone waving a white handkerchief. The handkerchief got smaller and smaller until it disappeared.

I do remember still being afraid. The part of Poland we moved to was Russian territory, and people were still being persecuted. My father disappeared, and we didn't know where he was. One day I was looking out of the window and I saw this man coming down the street, and I started screaming that my father was back. I recognized him immediately, even though he was so broken and thin. And I remember my mother crying and holding him. She didn't think she'd see him alive again. I still have no idea why the Communists arrested him or why they let him go. All I remember is that he came home broken. Not long after that my mother gave birth to another little boy. My aunt and the other women gave me my first doll, a rag doll, when he was born. I remember wondering whether the men would take him away, too, as they'd taken away my other baby brother. My mother must have weighed eighty pounds at this point, after the war and the birth of my brother, so they sent her to a sanitorium to recuperate. I don't remember being afraid, because she promised me that she would come back, and after several months she came home, having gained a lot of weight, all brown from the sun. She talked to me about how it had been like *Magic Mountain,* sitting covered up on a lounge chair all day in the snow, drinking gobs of milk. I was so glad to have her home.

I don't remember anything more until we moved to Valdenburg, which was on the German-Polish border, in a part that became Poland. Probably there was work there for my father. They assigned us this nice apartment, full of pretty things, and toys. Those were the first toys I ever had. There was a beautiful dollhouse with wonderful furniture and faucets with real water. I played with the toys, but they didn't seem real, I just went through the motions.

But we were always scared, that's what I remember, screams in the night and people being taken away. Once my parents and I were in the street and we witnessed a hanging. A young boy with a placard listing his crimes was standing on a truck with a noose around his neck tied to a tree. At the last second, my mother turned my head away, but I wanted to look, and I saw him hanged. I couldn't stand for anyone to touch my neck for a long time after that. Nothing had changed, basically, nothing was on firm ground in that Communist area. And that's why my father decided to cross the border to get to an American sector, and eventually to go to Palestine.

My brother must have been about a year old, so I was five, and my cousin Rachel was around four, when someone was hired to take us over the border. My parents didn't know whether we could trust him or not, whether he'd take our money and shoot us, but my father decided we had to take the risk. Whatever fear he had, he was more afraid to continue living in this unpredictable Communist climate than to risk death. My mother put my brother into his baby carriage and told me we were going for a walk. Everything we owned we left behind in this very pretty apartment, and we walked to the edge of town. It was twilight. My father met us there, and my uncles and aunt and a few other families joined us. Then this border person came and he gave sleeping pills to my brother. I remember hearing some talk among the adults that if he cried they would have to strangle him, suffocate him, because they couldn't risk the lives of all of us for one child. Even then it amazed me how little power we children had. We only had the choice of crying or not crying, but we had no power. So we were told not to cry under any circumstances, that it meant our lives.

We walked all night, not knowing whether this guide was going to turn on us and shoot us all, hoping that my brother wouldn't cry. He stayed awake all night staring at the moon and the stars, but he didn't cry. It was such a clear night you could see through the woods, and it was perfectly quiet except for the crunching of our feet against the ground. Every now and then my father picked me up and carried me, then put me back down again. We had left the carriage when we got to the woods and my mother held my brother in her arms. She had a pacifier and would stick it in a little sugar she had brought with her, then put it in his mouth. We walked this way over the border into Czechoslovakia.

Once we crossed the border there were groups waiting to help us. They fed us and cleaned us up, let us rest and get warm, and the next day put us on the train for Germany. It was a cattle car without a roof, a slop bucket over to one side to be used as a bathroom, and blankets over us to keep out the rain. It took three weeks riding this way to Ulm, Germany, the town where Einstein was born. Once we arrived, we went through a whole process then of delousing, examinations, sorting, cards, labels, document checks and rechecks. We stayed in barracks at first where there must have been fifty people sleeping in one room. I slept in one bed with my father, my brother slept in another with my mother. God, there were endless lines of people in Ulm, people waiting for food, for health checks, for clothing. All these ravaged-looking people in stunned surprise, blinking at the light, trying to figure out where they were now, what to adapt to next, asking each other, "Do you know . . . ? Have you heard of . . . ?"

Outside of the fenced-in area were other homes of Germans who had been displaced in order to make room for refugees. After the first few weeks, my father refused to continue to live behind the fence and found an apartment for us outside the camp, four families in one apartment with a room for each family and a shared kitchen and bath. My God, it felt luxurious. We had our own room with two beds and a closet, a table and chairs. I remember seeing how other people lived. Some were very elegant, even though they only had one room, because they came from elegant backgrounds and managed to convey that with little touches, a rug or a picture. My father painted flowers on our wall, which made me feel very secure and contented when I looked at them.

All the children went to school until after lunch. It was the first real school I'd ever attended and I was in the first grade. We had desks and ink and pens and notebooks, and half of the classes were held in Yiddish, half in Hebrew, since the camp was geared for immigration to Israel. There must have been thirty of us in each classroom from Russia, Romania, Poland and other parts of Germany. All of us learned language overnight by osmosis. I don't think we were even conscious of going from one language to another; it was part of being a chameleon, learning to adapt to whatever the environment forced onto us. My father felt it was relatively safe for me to run around and play close to our building. I have snapshots of me in our apartment, of me and my friends, of the school yard. But when I'd leave his sight, even to go to the bathroom, he'd always tell me to be careful. If I left the immediate neighborhood, it was traumatic for my father, he couldn't let me go. Crossing the border was the last risk he could permit me to take. Our school had a picnic planned up in the mountains. There were army trucks to take us, and I wanted to go on that outing more than anything, but my father wouldn't let me. My mother said, "You know she's got to go with the other children," and she took me to the truck and put me on it. Just when we were about to pull away, my father came and pulled me off. Maybe it was his guilt about buying the poison for me in the camp that was the problem.

It was a time of getting over the shock, or the shock setting in, I'm not sure which. My father became paralyzed. I don't know the diagnosis, whether it was psychological or physical, but he couldn't move at all. They had to pull all his teeth because he had a massive infection from malnutrition. He was like a dead man, and only his body remained. I tried to court him, to get him to laugh, to be interested in things. It was a never-ending battle to bring him back to life. On Purim in the DP camps, my mother made a real holiday of it. She got an embroidered piece of colored cloth to put on the table, fruit and wine and a candelabra, and she made homentachen and challah. My parents had a friend who had lost his entire family, and he came to our Purim party. It was his last supper, because after that night he killed himself. My father could have committed suicide, too; I'm not sure why he didn't. Eventually he could walk again, but he stayed dead inside; that never changed.

The adults' goal was to get out of the DP camp, out of Germany. Kids would come home and be told they were going to leave for Palestine or America or Canada or Australia. We got used to it, people waiting their turn to leave, and the preparations for moving on. But there were unexpected traumas. Rachel and I slept in the same bed in our apartment, One night she woke me up crying. There was blood coming out of her mouth, bright red on the pillow and she was terrified. They took her away to a sanitorium for tuberculosis, but I never saw her again. She died and I don't know what happened to her body; she simply disappeared as though she had never existed. Loss was a constant in the DP camp. The only thing that saved us children was that we were all in the same situation. I didn't feel different or odd.

My father's nephew had written to us through the Red Cross. He and his sister, children of the brother my father had lived with in Vienna, were living in the United States. They wrote, "Instead of going to Palestine, why don't you come to America?" I began having fantasies about what it would be like in America. I'd heard about streets of gold, and the cowboys, and I thought it would be absolutely fantastic. People said, "Oh, you're so lucky to be able to go there. I have a nephew in Chicago, maybe you can meet him." We had no idea about the sheer size of the place, or what a different kind of world this was. I would imagine getting off the boat with all these people asking me questions which I would answer and becoming friends. I'd already had some contact with America because children would send us Red Cross boxes. I can still smell the Palmolive soap they put in them. I have a color blown-up photograph of me wearing this absolutely exquisite dirndl dress my mother made for me, for this special occasion. She's a professional seamstress and she could pick up a rag and come up with a gorgeous dress. This day of the photograph they had set up a grandstand so each of us children could come up one by one and get our little packages filled with goodies. Then we would write thank-you letters to all those nice American children who had sent us perfumed soap and Ipana tooth powder. I remember getting two washcloths and thinking, "Now what in the world is this?" I'd never seen a washcloth before, or deodorant. We had laundry soap if we had anything. That's what I knew about America, Red Cross boxes with these wonderful smells floating out when they were opened. So I thought, I'm going to this country where all these boxes are readily available, and those children who sent me these gifts will want to be my friends. I was so excited about it all.

Part of the legacy I pass on is what happened to me during the Holocaust. That's bad enough, it's enough to have to deal with. But there's another part that happened after to me, what I thought of myself coming into a normal world, finding that world wanted no part of me. We left on the *SS Heinselmann*, with a wicker basket containing all our possessions: clothes, blankets, photographs and documents. We shared a cabin with another woman and her children. All the men had to sleep downstairs in the hold where the sailors had been, and they slept on hammocks, but the women and children had cabins with bunks. It was September and there were storms. When the weather was nice we sat outside on the deck on a blanket. I remember eating hard candies because that stopped seasickness, lime bonbons and round lemon ones. The night before we were due to land, nobody slept, and it was every bit as exciting as they had promised. My parents were crying and I was jumping up and down having spotted this enormous beautiful statue in the sea, thinking of the Red Cross boxes and friends. The skyline of Manhattan was like another planet.

We were going to Boston where my cousins lived. The trip took six, maybe seven hours, and my brother, who was then about four years old, began to act funny, but we didn't know what was the matter with him. We didn't know a word of English, and when we got to Boston, no one was there to meet us. I don't think my father even knew how to use an American telephone. It was late at night, and by this time my brother had a high fever, and we hadn't even gotten our land legs yet. We were totally bewildered and exhausted. My father settled us on a bench in the middle of this huge, teaming station with vaulted ceilings and foreign voices coming through loudspeakers, and he told my mother to stay there while he went to try to find my cousin. My mother was terrified. She didn't want to be left alone, and she had visions of his never returning, but there was no choice. After a few hours, he came back with my cousin, who took us to his house, which seemed to us like a palace, a two-story house just for one family. My brother had a pretty high fever by then, a serious case of measles, and had to be kept in a dark room, and we were quarantined with him at my cousin's. Actually, that gave us a good chance to recuperate before they moved us to our own apartment.

Our relatives lived on one side of Boston and our apartment was on another, like opposite ends of the world. That's when the isolation began for us, living in that one-bedroom apartment without English or living skills or jobs for my parents. Of all that happened to me during the war, that time in America was the worst. I was sent to a Hebrew school on a scholarship because I spoke fluent Hebrew after three years in the DP camp school. I hated it there, I was the pet refugee, and I had to really sing for my supper. They'd call me out of class to talk to visitors about where I came from and show off my wonderful Hebrew. And then came the big question, "How do you like America?" I had to say how much I loved it here, how grateful I was to be at that school. They didn't really want to hear that I felt like a dirty little refugee who wore other peoples' clothes and spoke with an accent and didn't understand the rules of the game. One day the teacher brought in this big box of combs, gloves, hats, and she pulled out a pair of gloves and said, "Who belongs to this?" I thought she was offering it, and I raised my hand. Then she picked out a hat, and I raised my hand again. Pretty soon the other kids caught on and started to laugh at me. I did not know what a Lost and Found was. When I started going to other children's houses, I was acutely aware of how different we were, and I had never felt different before, and had never been treated as though I weren't as good as everyone else. I remember being in the principal's office with another girl, and the other girl smelled dirty and sweaty. Someone came over to me and said, "You ought to take a bath more often, Anna." The assumption was that I was the refugee and I wasn't clean. Because it was an Orthodox school, I had to lie about not being observant in our home. We had no interest in religion and we didn't keep kosher, so I couldn't invite kids to my house because then they'd know. Doing things our own way wasn't acceptable, yet we couldn't really be part of the school. My parents didn't have a car and could never come to school functions because we lived so far away. No other parents ever invited them along. Clearly people were not very nice. I know I should be grateful, I know it sounds like I'm very bitter. I remember we didn't have a telephone for a long time because we couldn't afford one, so my mother went to a neighbor's house to ask if she could use their phone. I don't think she abused it, she didn't chitchat, she only asked when she needed it. But one day my mother went over and knocked on the door to ask if she could use the telephone. The woman got irate. "I'm sick and tired of you coming here," she said in Yiddish. "I don't want you to come back." She had a girl my age and we used to play together until that.

We looked like refugees, like greenhorns. One day my mother, my father, my brother, and I were walking down the street and we saw another family who looked just like us. My mother didn't hesitate one second before she went over to the woman and started talking to her in Yiddish, asking where they were from. They hugged and kissed and were so happy to see each other. The families became friends. It was nice having other people like us we could speak with in Yiddish. Mr. Sigoloff had a job, but one day he didn't come home from work and Mrs. Sigoloff called my father, because by that time, a couple of years after we'd been here, we did have our own phone. My father told her Mr. Sigoloff must have been delayed. But he didn't come and he didn't come, and finally they went to the place where he worked and found him hanging.

My mother got a job in the supermarket as a meat-wrapper. She's a very efficient woman and she stayed in that supermarket for many years. Eventually she became a manager. My father also worked there, but he went from job to job, and never quite made it. My mother always wanted to move out of that neighborhood, but my father was terrified to leave, he wanted to stay in that one-bedroom apartment forever. Finally, when I was a teenager and it was obvious that I needed my own room, my mother found a lovely two-bedroom garden apartment, but it was against my father's wishes that we moved. My father wasn't the only one depressed; my mother cried a lot and often withdrew. When she applied for compensation from Germany, my father refused. She said, "That's stupid, we deserve it, you know; we'll need the money to live on one day." She initiated the legal process for restitution money and had to go for an evaluation to a psychiatrist in Baltimore whose specialty was Holocaust survivors. I went with her because she needed a translator. This doctor wrote in his report that she functioned normally, which prevented her from getting the optimal amount of restitution money, and then he used her as a case study in the psychiatric literature. I found it by accident talking to a psychiatrist who referred to this doctor's work, and when I mentioned my mother, he said, "Oh, I know about her case." She was thinly enough disguised, so she could be recognized. I'll never forget that damned doctor. He wouldn't listen to her. He asked questions, but he wouldn't listen to the answers, and she needed so badly to talk with someone to help her deal with her losses and her grief. Yes, she was coherent, she wasn't demented or physically wasting away. She was working, taking care of her family, but he didn't want to know about the crying, or the fact that she would go for weeks without talking to anyone, or the headaches that were so severe that they debilitated her or that she woke up at night screaming from dreams about being chased, about people beating her up, about being so hungry that she would stuff anything into her mouth to stave off the hunger. And my father wouldn't talk about our experiences, although he had an opportunity to be a witness in one of the trials in Germany. They were going to pay his way because he knew the person being tried and why, but he wouldn't go back. He sent his written testimony instead.

When I was a child, I didn't really think consciously of exploitation, or a conspiracy of silence, or any of the things that haunt me now. I mean we survived, I went to school, I had friends, I adapted. But that was all surface. Under the surface I was afraid to sleep alone in a room until I was thirteen years old. I had nightmares, I never felt like I belonged, and I was acutely conscious of my parents' pain and confusion, and the fact that they couldn't talk about it. That's when I had my Riverdale fantasies. I'd read "Archie" in the comic strips and pretended that I came from Riverdale, too, just like Betty and Veronica, and lived in a big frame house with parents who were normal, who ate dinner with me at the table every night, a father who would go out to see a movie, who came to school functions, who drove a car, and all I had to worry about was what to wear to the Prom on Saturday night.

My father loved to read, and every Saturday he and I would go to the secondhand bookstores in Boston and browse. He'd go to the foreign language section, and I'd find other books to bring home. On a rare occasion I'd get him to go to the art museum with me, but not very often. He really needed me to get him out. When I went away to live at college, I knew I'd never be back again, and that was the hardest part. My father cried, he said, "How can you leave, you've got everything you need right here, you're close to your college, why do you have to live there?" The night before I left, I sat looking at his face, feeling terrible, knowing what separation meant to him. But I had to attend to my life, to choose Riverdale if I felt like it. I thought I was attached to a very long cord, to a very far past, and I could stretch the cord further and further, and eventually it would snap. My brother was a definite part of the family, but he was also out of the family. My mother and father and I had a special tie, a special dance we did together that excluded him. He never spoke Yiddish. We still speak in Yiddish, my mother and I. He never was as protected as I was, he could come and go as he pleased. He stopped going to Hebrew school and went on to public school. I never could. The only time my parents and I stopped dancing was when I finally left home, and even then it wasn't over.

I had a mission when I left home, to find a secure place for me in the world. I needed self-esteem, position; I needed to feel I was more than a dirty refugee. I wanted to create a perfect environment in which I could have children. Not just children, but miraculous children. I imagined conversations with them, games, trips, the life I never had as a child. I had that fantasy from the time before I had words for it. I met my husband the very first day I was in college, and he was clearly the smartest boy I had ever met. That night I called my mother and told her I had met the boy I was going to marry. I didn't even like him, I wasn't particularly attracted to him, except that I knew he was smart enough to be the father of my incredible children. I needed his genes, but I didn't necessarily want someone mucking around in my past, which is part of why I picked him, because he didn't want anything to do with my past either. That part of me I kept hidden away.

For the next four years, I had a passionate relationship with Reuben, even though we had no formal arrangement between us. I never veered from the notion of marrying him, though it was frequently painful, and always extreme. The irony of it was that I met another boy that year who was not Jewish, but who was my soul mate. I connected with him in ways I never could with Reuben. But at that time in my life, I couldn't allow myself to marry someone who wasn't Jewish. It was too soon after the war, and I couldn't do that to my parents. Reuben came from a rather wealthy family, they had lovely things, his mother was an artist. I had cultural advantages at my fingertips in our relationship, and he was extraordinarily intelligent, I had been right about that, After I finished college, I followed him to New York where he was in law school. I found a job, and Reuben introduced me to two women who were looking for a roommate. One was the daughter of a Nazi, and there was this instant repelling attraction between us. She had had as difficult a life as I had had. She had been raised in an orphanage, abused by nuns, her parents divorced, and her mother was an alcoholic, in addition to her father's Nazi soldier past. She was bright and extremely beautiful. The other roommate was a Polish non-Jew. The three of us settled into an apartment, three refugees. That was how my husband always saw me. Whenever he'd get mad at me, he'd yell, "You with that lousy refugee mentality!" It was a perfect relationship he'd provided for me with that German girl. She had to atone for what her father had done, and I needed someone to do the atoning. But she had violent rages, and there were more and more times I was terrified to be alone with her in the apartment. Finally I moved in with Reuben because I was so afraid of her. After I'd been out of our apartment for a few days, there was a news story on the radio about a girl who had committed suicide. It was my roommate. She had taken barbiturates and alcohol, and had called the police because she got scared, but by the time they got there she was in a coma and they couldn't revive her. I didn't go to the funeral. I felt so guilty, I thought maybe if I hadn't come into her life, she wouldn't have killed herself. I was furious with her. She had the last argument. I didn't like her, I didn't want to be with her, I was glad when she died, and I felt terrible.

After that, one day during my lunch hour, Reuben and I went to City Hall and got married. There was no other choice, I didn't know where else to go. I spent my wedding night alone because Reuben had work to do. There was no feeling of joy, but a sinking feeling of, "Oh, now what have I done?" But that went away quickly thinking about the life I could create for my children. The only flaw was that my husband didn't really want me or any children. Even in the early months he was never there physically or emotionally for me, but I needed to do everything in my power to make my marriage work, to create my dream children. During this time I had a friend, a man who saw me as intelligent, more than just a refugee. I still see him, twenty-two years later we are still friends. I was extremely grateful to him for helping to hold my marriage together during that time, for giving me what support my husband couldn't.

After Reuben got his law degree, we moved to Philadelphia. It was time for the next phase, to have a baby. We had been married a couple of years. It didn't take long for me to get pregnant, but my husband was furious when he found out, though he knew full well I'd been trying. I hadn't drugged him, he had participated, but the reality overwhelmed him. He said it was the stupidest thing I could have done, and he was ranting and raving. I left the house and wandered around, afraid to go back home. Here I was carrying my first child, and my husband didn't want either of us. I should have left him then. When I had the baby, he wasn't even at the hospital. He had gone to trial, even though he could have postponed it. I remember my panic at the thought that he'd run away.

After my daughter was born, I had this terrible fear that my husband wasn't the father of the baby, even though I hadn't slept with anybody else. I was terrified that he'd find out and leave me. That fear haunted me for a month. I must have been thinking about the men who had been my spiritual lovers when my husband wasn't, feeling guilty about those intimacies. Reuben wasn't a good father; he didn't spend time with our daughter, she was clearly my baby. The only wonderful part was that my parents were delirious with joy. It was the only time I was able to make my father happy. They moved to an apartment near us. Then, when the baby was a year and a half old, my father started speaking strangely, not remembering things. I thought he'd had a stroke. About six weeks later he died, though we never knew what he died of. It seemed so unfair that he should die at age sixty-seven, just when they were beginning to have a normal life.

I needed to have another baby, and this time my husband was happy about it. To this day, my second child is his favorite, the perfect child, intelligent, beautiful, nondemanding. Reuben was even there at her birth, and I began to think that our lives might work out. We had some property in Maine, right on the ocean, with a house that was built in 1920, where we could take the children. But my husband went into the army and we had to move again, this time back to Boston. The area we moved to was beautiful, but there were no women my age, no young families, and I was at home all day with two children under the age of four. It was physically painful, that time in my life, I couldn't breathe with the pain. I went to a psychiatrist who started to help me delve into my past, but he was so distant, and I needed so much. I felt myself spiraling into my past, which I couldn't handle. Over Christmas my psychiatrist left town, and I knew I had hit bottom. I couldn't get out of bed and started crying and couldn't stop. My husband called a doctor who was taking my doctor's calls, and he said I needed to be hospitalized.

My husband dropped me off at the hospital and took the children to Pittsburgh to stay with his sister. Without a suitcase or clothes or my house keys, I checked myself in. I was in a daze, but when they took me up to the psychiatric ward and locked the door behind me, I knew I had made a terrible mistake. I didn't belong there, I needed to get ahold of myself, to stop spiraling. They brought me liquid Thorazine, which burned so badly I thought my head was going to burst into flames, and in a couple of hours I was a zombie. It was hard to think about how I could get out of that ward, but I knew I was going to get out. I had been in the darkness too many years in my past, and the fear of going back there pulled me out of it.

I had one quarter in my purse, and I called a girlhood friend who lived near the hospital. I told her to call the airlines and make a reservation for me to go to Pittsburgh, and to have her husband come get me. I told her I'd pay her back for the plane tickets, but please, I needed her help. When her husband came, the nurses didn't want to let me go, but I had signed myself in, so there was nothing they could do to keep me there. They handed me the Thorazine and told me to take it every four hours. By that time, I had developed full-blown Parkinsonian symptoms. I was shuffling and shaking, and I had no control over my tongue. When I got to Pittsburgh, I gave the cab driver my sister-in-law's address. I said I didn't have any money, but my relatives would pay him when we got there. My husband was furious when he saw me pull up to the door. "What are you doing here? You belong in the hospital, you can't take care of the children!" I said it had been a mistake, that I had to go home, that I needed rest. We called my mother in Israel, and she flew back to Boston. She took charge of our house and the children, threw open the shades, and let me sleep. Eventually I told my husband that we had to move, to a find a place to live where there would be people my age around so I wouldn't be so isolated, and that one time he came through for me. We found a neighborhood with other young families, and my mother moved in with us. She had her own apartment, which we added on, with a separate entrance. After that, she was always there for the children, except for the part of every year she went to live in Israel. She was more like a second mother than a grandmother.

It became easier for me to get on with my life. I got paralegal training and worked in the brokerage field for a while, then as a coordinator for a volunteer program in an agency. That was when I realized I wanted to become a social worker. I got involved with the women's movement and became very active, joined a consciousness group and really began looking at myself. I think of that period in my life as my birth, because my life was never the same after that. I've never been that depressed again. My children were still my dream children; one was reading at eighteen months, one had a gift for music. We spent time at our house in Maine, and I planned these marvelous trips every year. Then we moved to Rhode Island and I got a job. I saved every penny for these trips, one more glorious than the next, that I arranged and paid for. It was one adventure after another with the children, they were such marvelous travelers. They slept on the floor sometimes and reveled in seven-course meals.

One year we went through Germany. I was planning to stay a couple of days to show my children around, but there was an air strike and we couldn't get out, although my husband found one seat for himself on a charter airline and left us there, with masses of people milling around, hundreds sleeping on benches. I started shaking and couldn't stop, couldn't think, couldn't move, trapped in this German-speaking environment with no way to get out. Fortunately my son was old enough to take over. But no one reached out to me in the way that I needed, to talk about my past. When we were in Israel, I wanted to go to Yad Vashem. I asked my husband to go with me, but he refused. I went by myself on a bus and walked into this one museum that is dark except for an everlasting flame, with slabs of stone around the room, representing each of the concentration camps. All around me were people, but I was the only one alone, and I felt myself standing on the edge of a well, trying to catch myself from slipping in. I started to cry, and I hated Reuben for not being there. He never asked me how it was, if I was all right. Now I realize that he felt trapped with me and my children. I do say my children, because at the time he didn't intrude on our relationship, and maybe I didn't want him to. I was afraid of him; his quick wit and sarcasm were barbs that made bull's-eyes every time. I tried to protect the children from his abuse. I was terrified that Reuben would leave me. I needed a family to define myself. There were times when I'd look in the mirror and there would be no image.

Eventually we moved to Chicago, where I found a house we loved. I took great pleasure thinking that there had been a family living in this beautiful old house while I was hidden in an attic in Poland. They didn't even know it wasn't their house, that they were just keeping it for me. I got a scholarship to graduate school in Chicago, and I continued emerging. Jobs were always offered to me, but I started to have problems with my kids, and I felt lonelier and lonelier in my marriage, without family or friends I had left behind in Boston. I began to wish that I could go back to the way I was before my marriage; to friends who thought of me as exotic, wearing a trenchcoat, smoking cigarettes, leaning against a lamppost like a heroine from a grainy black and white movie from the thirties, meeting for Tanqueray martinis in a cafe, talking about the past. I wanted to be with people who loved my past. I attended a conference that started me thinking about what had happened to me as a child, about how I'd tried to pretend the Holocaust wasn't my experience and denied myself any credibility in my own eyes. What I've needed to come to terms with was that being a survivor doesn't only mean feeling dirtied by experiences and discounted, it means being a winner, too. I wish it hadn't happened, I feel annoyed about my past, I don't like it, I could have done without it. Time doesn't sit still, time doesn't lie flat. It's not "point A" and "point B" with "A" in the past and "B" in the future. Sometimes time comes loose, moves and undulates and touches on itself. Sometimes I'm here and sometimes I'm there, and I travel back and forth in time, as I think all Holocaust survivors do.

I was married for twenty-two years, and recently my husband walked out on me. He's involved with another woman, and I'm furious. I feel like all that I worked for he's taken away. I have to sell my house and I have no idea what my future will bring. I can't leave Chicago for two more years, until my daughter finishes high school, but I know how important family is to me, and whatever relatives I have left in Boston, I need to be near them. I feel like I'm in suspended animation until I go back East, until I can connect with someone who loves me. I don't know if I have the capacity to be truly intimate with a man, to allow someone to be so powerful that he'll have the capacity to make me happy, or to hurt me. I gave up the chance for that once when I was in college because the boy I loved wasn't Jewish. My ex-husband is very angry with me, but he's always been an angry man. Maybe that was the only kind of intimacy I could have had then. Love and tenderness make me vulnerable. I'm scared and lonely now, but I feel impatient to get on with life. Life is so short, and we're dead for such a long time.

2
Kayla

Kayla was born into an Orthodox Jewish family in a small town in Poland. As her parents became more aware of the impossibility of surviving as Jews, her mother took her to another small town in Poland where they changed their names and lived as Catholics. She was two years old when her identity changed, ten years old when her family moved to Belgium and began to reestablish themselves as Jews. Because of the secrecy and confusion she experienced as a child, it is essential for Kayla to examine what is happening to her and why. She expressed her need for knowing where she stands symbolically in her fear of dusk, "that in-between time, not light and not yet dark." She did not want to continue living in the dark about herself, not knowing who she is and where she belongs. For too many years she was in between Christianity and Jewishness, in between having a father and not having a father, in between being a survivor and being the child of survivors. Her return to Orthodoxy as an adult living in the United States is a return to her past, those years she has always been told she was "too young to remember." At the end of our final session, Kayla said she wanted to pay me for all that she learned about herself through our interviews. I told her that she paid me well by giving me her story.

They say that the first six years of a child's life are the most important psychologically. The first time I read this, I said to myself, *boy, I must be messed up,* because the first six years of my life I had no idea who my father was or where I came from, or why I was taught to lie. I've never talked to anyone before about my past, even my husband doesn't know the whole story. When you put into perspective what happened to other people, I went through the war like a song. I never starved, I always had clothes on my back. Do you want to call it luck, or fate, or do you want to call it God? I asked myself why did I survive? Was I intended for some purpose, or perhaps my children are and I don't know it yet. When American Jews who never lived through the war have questioned me about my background, I feel as though I have to justify my existence, and yet I've been told so often, "Well, you were so young, you couldn't remember anything. The Holocaust didn't touch you, you were too young to understand." Older survivors in their sixties and seventies, my parents' age, don't really want to hear what I do remember. It's as though none of it happened to me, as though I'm still a little girl making up stories. I don't fit in with children of survivors either, I'm somewhere in the middle. When I saw your ad in the Jewish paper, looking for women who were very young children living in Europe during the Holocaust, I almost couldn't believe it. For the first time I thought, this is me, this is who I am, and someone wants to hear what I have to say.

I was born in 1940 in Tarnov, a small town in Poland. From what I gather, it's a town that was 50 percent to 60 percent Jewish. My parents both came from very Orthodox families, my father from another small town, my mother from Tarnov, although my mother had joined a Zionist organization and moved to Israel for a year, until her mother got sick and she came home to Poland. Then she met my father and they got married in 1939, the year Hitler invaded Poland. When I think about my parents, what I feel is so confusing. I need them to fill in the details of what I don't remember about my past, or never knew, and my father is more than willing to talk about the Holocaust. In fact, you can't be in the same room for five minutes without hearing about it. So I asked him to make some tapes for me, to have for my children. But when I listened to the first tape my father made, I heard something that shook me to the very core of my being. I'd known for a long time that when Germany invaded Poland, my mother was pregnant with me. I don't know how many months along she was, but she wanted to have an abortion, and there was a lot of talk back and forth, weighing the decision. Logically, it makes sense that she would have wanted to abort a child at that time, but my grandparents were very religious and were very much against abortions. They also felt it was dangerous because she was so far along, and with the bombings at the time, the procedure would have been risky. But what really shook me up when I listened to that tape was that my father said that a lot of young people in Poland went to Russia when Hitler came, and . . . I don't know why I'm crying . . . I'm sorry . . . my father said they couldn't go to Russia because my mother was pregnant . . . and, oh God, . . . if it hadn't been for me she might have escaped all of this. That upsets me more than the idea of not being born . . .

By the time I was born, Poland was already occupied. Jews were forced by German law to give up many things, including fur coats and jewelry, but my grandfather and father had a jewelry business and managed to hide some valuables, even though they had to leave their apartment and life in the ghetto area of Tarnov. My grandparents on both sides were deported, and there were rumors that the whole ghetto was going to be closed down eventually, everyone sent away. My parents speak about my grandfather as though he were a hero, a tzaddik . . . and he adored me . . . and I want to cry again, but I can't even tell you why . . . Since I've started talking about all of this to you, the stories I heard growing up that always sounded like they had happened to someone else's family and didn't connect with my life, they've changed, they belong to me. They were my grandparents who were murdered.

While we were living in the ghetto, a truck of German soldiers came to take the children away. The parents weren't told where the children would be taken, or forced to give them up, but some of the adults hoped the children would be better off going, I suppose, because they gave them willingly over to the Germans. I was about two years old then, and I don't remember, but they told me they put me on the truck with the other children . . . I'm sorry, here I go again . . . I started screaming and crying and kicking, and they said I wouldn't stop. Finally, a soldier picked me up and asked whose child I was, and my parents said I belonged to them, and this soldier said, "Take your little girl, if you're smart; keep her with you." And he handed me down to them. I can't imagine that they almost sent me away. I'm a mother, and I'd do anything to protect my children . . . it makes me angry now, for the first time, to think about this, that they almost had me killed. How many times as I was growing up my parents said I was "snatched from the claws of Hitler."

But then my father came up with a plan for saving my mother and me. There was a group of Jews whom my father knew from Tarnov who were living in Warsaw and had set up a network providing false ID papers, birth certificates, baptism records, and hiding Jews as Christians in the population at large. There was a Polish farmer who was a friend of my father's, an acquaintance of the family, and this Polish non-Jewish farmer took my mother and me out of the [Tarnov] ghetto to Warsaw. One day we just walked out, leaving my father behind because he looked too Jewish, and because his Polish wasn't very good. So it would have been clear that he was Jewish. This non-Jewish farmer acted as a go-between, bringing news of my father, along with jewelry to sell on the black market so my mother could get us food stamps in Warsaw. And this man, Marion, never took a cent for all he did for us, not a cent. He brought us butter and bread and eggs, and my mother would invite him to sit down with us, and he'd say, "No, Hannah, I brought this food for you and the child." There really were some good people during the war. I knew that this man existed, and as a child, I took such kindness for granted.

For my mother it was a totally foreign world, trying to live in Warsaw as a Christian when she had been raised in an Orthodox Jewish family. She didn't know how to behave or what to say. The contacts who provided us with the false papers were like mentors for her and educated her about her Christian environment. Especially what to do about one major problem, and that problem was me . . . I can't . . . excuse me, I have to go get a cigarette. . . .

I'm sorry I get so wound up about this, but I was once again the problem. How do you tell a two-year-old who'd been brought up Jewish, keeping kosher, lighting the candles, saying prayers, how do you tell a two-year-old all of a sudden that she has to go to church and change within one day, change her entire way of living, who she is? How do you explain that her father disappeared from her life so suddenly? How do you expect a child not to be confused? To keep such important secrets? We had to change apartments a couple of times in Warsaw because the landlady would talk to all the children, and once she asked, "Hello, what's your name, where do you come from?" And I told her, "Well, I'm Catholic, but I'm really Jewish." Luckily, instead of going to the Gestapo, she went to my mother and said we couldn't live there anymore. My mother had to get a whole new set of papers, because even though our landlady didn't report us, my mother was afraid that she'd change her mind, so we changed our name again and we started over in a room in another apartment. My mother invented a background for us, saying that her husband was in the Polish army and was missing, and no one suspected any different, although the man who was her mentor told her I was becoming too Jewish looking, with dark hair and my father's Semitic features. He told her she should leave me in the apartment when she went out to the market, because in any public place the Germans might begin to question my appearance. He told her not to bring me to his house, either, when she came to visit, because I might put him in danger. So from that time on, she left me alone when she went out, and when she came back home I'd be crying, terrified of being all alone. I was drilled to say the Lord's Prayer every morning and every night, and we went to church every Sunday. Actually, I loved church. My mother would stay in the back, but I would always push and go in front because I wanted to be right there to see what was happening at the altar. I thought church was beautiful, and I was becoming an ardent Catholic. Then one day when I was around three years old, my father showed up at our room, as suddenly as he'd disappeared from my life. Only my mother didn't tell me he was my father, she said he was her husband's brother, my uncle, and he'd come to visit.

My father had heard the entire ghetto was going to be exterminated and had gotten a streetcar conductor's uniform and a bicycle to make his escape. The population, including the German soldiers, had a great respect for uniforms. It didn't make any difference what kind of a uniform, it didn't have to be a soldier's, as long as it was official, nobody bothered you, nobody asked for your ID, you were assumed to be part of the establishment. So with his conductor's uniform and a bicycle, my father went to Marion, got our address, and showed up at the hotel where we were living. It was hard for me to get used to having him with us. We were afraid he would be recognized as being Jewish if he lived with us and people got to know him too well, so he would come to visit us in his uniform, looking very official, and then he would wave goodbye, making sure everybody knew he was leaving. Then, after dark, he'd sneak back into our apartment. We had this big closet, and this was where he lived for a year and a half. When nobody was around, he could come out into our room. It was like a hotel where we lived, with other rooms off the hallway that led to our room. If I wanted to go out, I motioned to my uncle to go behind the cabinet so that if I opened the door, nobody would find him there. And if he had to go to sell something, he would leave very early in the morning when nobody was around and then come back as though he were just visiting when it was daylight. I was taught to lie very efficiently because it was drilled into me that there was nobody living in the apartment except my mother and me. My mother would wake me up in the middle of the night and say, "Who do you live with?" And I would say, "I live just with you; that's it, just with my mother alone." Other things, too, I was drilled to lie about. My uncle managed to buy things to eat on the black market that weren't available to the general population. When I played outside, I would beg for butter just like the other kids, even though I knew that in our house I could have butter or jam if I wanted. I lived two lives: in the outside world I had to behave in a certain way, but inside was totally different. And every time I went outside to play, my mother was so anxious until I got back. And then she'd drill me: "Now, what did you talk about? What did your friend ask you? What did you say?" The German soldiers weren't looking for Jews who lived as non-Jews, but there were all kinds of rewards for turning Jews in, and therefore all kinds of spies. The Polish population was just as anti-Semitic, if not more so, than the Germans, and they were more than happy to turn somebody in. My parents' lives were basically in my hands.

My mother remembers when the Warsaw ghetto was fighting back, the comments of all the people around. She couldn't let on how she was feeling. And I remember, I think it was 1944, the Russians were at the river in front of Warsaw and the partisans started an uprising. The Russians didn't want the partisans in the way after the war. They wanted the power for themselves. So the Russian soldiers stopped at the river, and in their infinite wisdom, let the Germans slaughter the partisans for them. There was a lot of fighting in the city and we were supposed to go down into the basement during the air raids. My mother had to leave my uncle upstairs because he wasn't supposed to be living there. But the neighbors started kidding her about this brother-in-law of hers who came to visit, because my father is a very friendly, likable guy, and they felt sorry for my mother who was alone, and they started telling her that she should ask her brother-in-law to move in with her. That allowed my uncle to live openly and to be down in the cellar with us after that. I remember going down on the floor and bullets whizzing in through the open window at night.

The Germans systematically bombed Warsaw. The soldiers went from house to house, emptied all the buildings, and then blew them up. I remember that. I remember the German soldiers standing at the door and us being herded like cattle out of the city, Jew or non-Jew, it was a matter of survival. We walked to a little village outside of Warsaw and found shelter with farmers. Most of the Polish farmers didn't know how to read or write and were very primitive in their ways of living, although they were very good-hearted about taking us in, my uncle, my mother and myself. My uncle worked in the fields, and my mother helped, too. At that point it didn't really matter that my uncle's Polish wasn't so good, or that he looked Jewish, because the farmers were so unaware of the world, although they had heard of Jews from the stories they told. My uncle went with the guys to the pub, drinking, and he told me once they were talking about another farmer whose pigs were so nice and fat because they were Jewish pigs. Some Jews had come as runaways and had found shelter with this farmer, who called the Gestapo. The soldiers came right away and shot the Jews, then buried them right there on the farm. When it got dark, the farmer uncovered the corpses and fed them to his pigs, so that's how they got to be such nice, fat pigs. With stories like these, even though this family was so generous, there was no doubt in my parents' mind that if there were any suspicion that we were Jews, we wouldn't be alive for one more minute.

The everyday problem of bathing was monumental, because everything was done in this common room, and in those days no male was circumcised except Jews. My uncle had to invent reasons to go out to the river to wash. He became a celebrity because even in the fierce winter, he would go and crack the ice and swim in the river. He was such a young, strong man, the farmer we lived with was most impressed. He had two daughters and tried to talk my uncle into marrying one of them, which forced my uncle to come up with a plausible excuse for refusing without offending the farmer or making him suspicious.

Eventually the Russians liberated Poland. I remember the Russian planes flying overhead, and everybody yelling and waving. My father and all the other farmers were stone drunk, singing and laughing. Then we were free to leave the farm. I remember going to the train station. Everybody was going somewhere, even though there weren't many trains running. But I remember it was dusk and I was afraid of getting lost, afraid of the people yelling and screaming and trying to get onto the trains. Sometimes even now when I'm traveling someplace and it's that in between time, not light and not yet dark, I get this fear in me. Once, when I was fifteen or sixteen years old, I was walking in downtown Frankfurt, and there were a lot of people rushing back and forth. It was just getting dark and I got so panicky all of a sudden, and I couldn't understand where that came from. As recently as a few weeks ago, I was driving someplace and it was dusk, the sky with funny little clouds, and I was getting that old feeling back, and I remembered that scene when I was a child, and I said to myself, "Well, you're still not over that."

It was May of '45 when we went to the city of Lodz and rented an apartment. I got extremely sick with typhus or typhoid, one of the two. Whatever I had was very contagious and the doctor wanted to take me to the hospital to be quarantined, but my mother refused to let me go. She claimed the conditions in the hospital after the war weren't adequate. Instead she locked herself up in the room with me and wouldn't let anyone in except the doctor for a week or two until I was well. In the meantime, my uncle went to Sopok, a city up north near Danzig, where he had heard there were possibilities for rebuilding a life. Throughout my childhood, my mother worried about my health. It was as though she couldn't believe that I was alive, even to this day.

My mother didn't hear anything from my uncle after he left us behind, and she got very concerned and decided to try to find him. We met him in the train station by luck, just when he was coming back to get us. He had found a demolished jewelry store among all the ruins of the city of Sopok, and all the equipment for casting jewelry. He took us back with him to an apartment where a German couple took us in. My uncle's store was the first one rebuilt in Sopok, and he became the bigshot in town. My parents still did not make it known even to me that we were Jewish, although one day they told me they had learned that my father died and my mother and my uncle had married, but I never saw any ceremony. We had a beautiful apartment, and my mother hired a young girl to take care of me and a nurse for my brother when he was born in 1946. I still wanted to go to church some days, but my mother stopped going herself and sent me to mass with the maid.

The communists started to take over in 1946, and my father, as the biggest capitalist in town, was being blackmailed by the tax people. They kept telling him he owed money, no matter how much he paid, and it was a matter either of paying up, or else . . . And he could see there was no end to this, he had to join the party, which he had no intention of doing, or he had to get out. So, in 1947, we left Poland to go to South America, with a stopover in Belgium. Brazil was a place where a lot of Jews went after the war, and my father had a distant cousin in Brussels where we were supposed to stay only a short time. There were no explanations to me about any of this. I was simply told we were going and I was used to being a good girl, not questioning or complaining, simply doing as I was told.

Our financial status changed drastically when we went to Brussels. We lived in a two-room apartment and there was no talk of maids or nurses. My father had a hard time working because he wasn't a citizen, and in addition, he had bought pounds sterling which turned out to be counterfeit silver made by Hitler in an attempt to destroy the economy of England. But my parents decided to stay in Brussels since we had relatives there. By this time I was seven years old. The evening before I went to school for the first time, my parents sat me down in the kitchen, my brother was sitting in my mother's lap, and they told me that I was Jewish, that they were Jewish, too, and so were my grandparents, all our family. Jewish, I thought, and I remembered all those stories I had heard about Jews. I remembered walking with this young woman who was taking care of me after the war in Poland. Two men had passed us and she had said to me, "Those look like Jews." And I looked at them, too, thinking they were like creatures from outer space. Now I was one of those.

When we had left Poland, some people had given me this gorgeous white and gold Catholic catechism book. After my parents told me all the lies I had never known, I went to my room and ripped that book to shreds. I had so many questions, every day, it took me a long time for this to sink in. I started telling tall tales in school about having an older sister who was killed by a dog. For years and years my mother had to unteach me to lie. I had been trained to lie to everyone, and my mother had lied to me about my father, about being Catholic. I didn't know the difference between a lie and the truth. And it was so difficult for me to accept my father. I was afraid of him. He was never home, always working, or arguing with my mother about wanting to move to Frankfurt where he said he could make a better living. My mother said Germany was no place for us to live, no place to raise a Jewish child, but in 1951 we moved and I was sent to a boarding school for French army children living in Germany, forty or fifty miles away from Frankfurt.

I was eleven years old and I got homesick, I remember that. In the whole school there were only two other Jewish children, two girls who became my really close friends. They called us the three musketeers. I was so much more comfortable with them than the other army brats. But eventually my parents took me out of that boarding school so I could live at home and go to school nearby, which was German. Germans made me uncomfortable, whether I just felt it on my own or inherited my mother's anxiety, I'm not sure. There was only one other Jewish girl in my school of about a thousand students, and she was very different from me. She ran away from home when she was seventeen or eighteen, eloped with a boy because her parents did not approve of him. I was the little wallflower, the goody-goody. The adults talked about the fact that this girl's parents had been killed, that her father was really her uncle who had adopted her, that she'd been hidden in some attic for a couple of years during the war, but all of this was hearsay from my parents. She and I never discussed our experiences. Even my two close friends at boarding school never talked about our background. I was told so often, "Oh, you were too young, you don't remember," so I just assumed they couldn't remember either or didn't want to talk about it. Whatever had happened during the war was the adults' right to talk about, not ours. In school, of course, the war was never mentioned. History stopped before World War I. I remember being surrounded in the hall of my German school by a group of girls who were questioning me about Judaism. I was the only Jew around and I felt like I had to protect myself and my religion from attack.

Around 1953, a young Orthodox man was sent from Israel to be a youth leader, to try to bring some togetherness to those of us Jewish children left after the war. I was the oldest of a group of five or six children who met on Shabbat afternoons to learn Hebrew songs and dances and talk about Israel. My parents also engaged a private tutor for me at this time in Germany, to teach me how to read Hebrew. And my mother introduced me to stories from the Old Testament. My formal religious education wasn't at all extensive, but my mother was a very strong Zionist and she encouraged me to read Herzl and Weizmann, and she talked about her Jewish heroes, who became my heroes. My father talked a great deal during that time about how it had been before the war, living as Orthodox Jews, lighting the candles on Friday night, keeping kosher, about his father, whom he worshipped. They made it possible for me to love the way of life I'd left when I was so small and gave me something to hold onto.

Still, my teenage years were very lonely. My parents would have died if I would have dated a German, but those were the only boys I met. It would have been like consorting with the enemy. I remember sitting home on Sunday afternoons, cutting out pictures of American movie stars from magazines. My parents wanted to take me with them visiting, but I didn't want to go with them, I wanted to be with people my own age, and there really wasn't anybody, since all of the Jewish children were younger. I wanted to get out of Germany, to go to the United States. But I was only sixteen years old and my mother was afraid to send me so far away. She decided to send me to a Jewish school in England, but when my mother and I got there, we both hated it, so she found another school, an international school for girls from all over, wealthy daughters of diplomats and political heads of state. Although I was the only Jew there, I was perfectly comfortable. I'd been brainwashed not to associate with Germans, but other non-Jews were fine. And being different at that school was the norm. I made friends from all over the world, India, Turkey, and Greece. I remember being homesick a bit, writing home every day, but being with girls my age, friends, outweighed everything. I worked very hard because I combined two years of work into a one-year program to finish high school and get a certificate in English at the same time. The headmistress of the school was worried that I couldn't handle this, taking French, Latin, history, and math at the same time as a separate course in English for foreigners, but I knew I could. Later she wrote to me that I was the only one that year who passed all of her exams.

After that, I went back to Germany, to live at home and go to school at the University of Frankfurt, although I still had it in mind that I would go on to college in America. I was always afraid of the male faculty in Germany, particularly one professor who wore boots and looked exactly like a Nazi. My parents took me on a trip to Paris, as a bribe to keep me in school in Germany another year. But after my second year, I wrote to several universities in the United States. I had made up my mind, I was nineteen years old and I was leaving. At that time, there were a great many American soldiers in Germany, and I was used to seeing them, although I thought girls who dated GIs were loose, since everyone knew that the guys had only one thing on their minds and would be here today, gone tomorrow. But a lot of the Jewish girls went to services Friday night on the army base, just to meet the Jewish American soldiers. A friend of mine called me the day after I got back from Paris and asked me to go to services with her, but it really was distasteful to me to use religion just to meet boys, so I wouldn't go. Even when some business friends of my father's told me about the new Orthodox Jewish rabbi, the chaplain in town, I wouldn't go meet him. I told my father's friend if that young rabbi wanted to meet me, he should call me up. He didn't call, but one night this girlfriend phoned me and she said there was a GI who wanted to meet a girl who could speak English, and I was the only one she knew, and please, at least could I go out with him once as a favor to her. I said he could come for dinner to our home, and my parents and I would sort of look him over. He turned out to be a nice young man, and after dinner he said that he'd made plans to double-date to the movies, if that was all right with me. It turned out that the Jewish rabbi I'd heard about was the double date. He was so quiet and nice, I was totally shocked when the next day he called. We began dating, but it seemed really ironic for me to be going out with a rabbi considering my background, and the only rabbi I had ever known was an old man, very wise, but authoritarian. I wasn't sure how human Dan could be. He was Orthodox, and he knew I did not come from an observant background, which didn't seem to bother him. He never once asked me to adopt his practices, but from our very first date, just out of respect for him, I began to keep kosher when we were together. And since I went with him to services on Friday nights, I started observing the Sabbath, not driving or spending money. My father laughted at first, "Just because you're dating a rabbi doesn't already make you a rebbetzin." But it was more than just wanting to please Dan, it felt to me like I was returning to my past, picking up where I had been forced to leave off those years during the war. It felt totally natural for me to be an Orthodox Jew. It was the same spiritual feeling I had loved when I was Catholic going to church, and maybe from before that in Poland in our Orthodox home. By the time Dan and I discussed marriage two months later, there was nothing left to change in my religious practices. My mother was terribly worried about our decision to get married. I was only nineteen years old, and she didn't know Dan's family, although it was clear that he was from a different world. She was very afraid that twenty years later I'd blame religion for our problems. But I wasn't the least worried. I knew I wanted Dan, although I was uncomfortable about becoming a rebbetzin. I wasn't sure I could cope with being put in the limelight. Because of the circumstances in which I was raised, I had always been told to keep quiet, not to talk too much to strangers, and had become reticent about meeting people or socializing.

Dan and I met in April, and we were engaged by June. I was still a minor and needed my parents' permission to get married. When I brought the forms home for them to sign, they really dragged their feet. I told them it wasn't going to help, with or without their permission I was going to marry Dan, even if we had to wait two years. Shortly after we were married, I dropped out of school to travel with Dan on special assignments. I didn't want him touring Europe without me, but in doing that, I gave up any opportunity to be with people as my own person and became "the chaplain's wife." I had to watch out what I said, how I behaved, be friendly with everybody. People were nice, but there was no privacy. I had to entertain, smile, no matter how I felt. We were like the first family. My world in those days totally centered around Dan. His worries were my worries, and I was perfectly content with this. My goal in life was to totally submerge myself under his wishes. This was due, in part, to the European concept of a wife, and the role model my mother provided, although she was unhappy with it. I believed that a wife's job was to be the husband's support system, with no personality of her own. In fact, when our first child was born, the first Friday night out of the hospital, as soon as we sat down to dinner, the baby started crying and I was terribly upset because I couldn't give my full attention to Dan. I didn't want his routine to be disturbed because there was a baby in the house, and I made sure that didn't happen. When he came home at noon, lunch was waiting; at five o'clock, the table was set and dinner was ready. Dan got an extension of his three-year tour of duty and we stayed in Frankfurt until 1963. Our second child, Steffa, was three months old when we came to the United States, and Aaron was two years old. For a few weeks we lived with my mother-in-law. I had met her once, when she came to Germany for our wedding, but the relationship was not a good one, and moving to the same city in the United States where Dan's relatives lived didn't make the transition easy. He was the darling of the family, and I was the outsider, not a college graduate, and definitely not his mother's choice as a daughter-in-law.

We got an apartment in New York, where Dan was going to chaplains' school, not far from his family. None of the other chaplains' wives were Jewish, and I was stuck at home with two small children while Dan worked day and night. I felt really isolated. No matter where I went I was the outsider and it was Dan's territory. For the first time I became unhappy simply doing things for others, although I never verbalized my discontent. I felt Dan had a right to expect certain things of me. "Don't complain, you're the lucky one to be married to him," everyone said. Dan is a wonderful man. If he weren't, I wouldn't have wanted him. But he's human and no one wanted to recognize this. I felt more and more that I was being swallowed up in Dan's life.

Eventually we were transferred to Rhode Island, where I had more breathing space from his family's scrutiny. But I began to resent all the women that Dan dealt with as a rabbi and chaplain. Clergy are attractive to women, and it bothered me tremendously because I felt inadequate, like a poor little Polish orphan in comparison to sophisticated, educated, good-looking American women. Dan would mention, just in passing, how bright and intelligent so-and-so was, and I became jealous of every woman Dan talked with, since all I had to talk about was diapers and formulas, my unstimulating little world. There was a small college nearby, and to save my sanity I enrolled in a sociology class. It was no longer enough just to be Dan's alter ego, I wanted to contribute something of my own.

At that point Dan was with a MASH unit. Every once in a while he was called on an alert, which had become routine for us. But one day he was called and didn't come back. I didn't know where his unit went, they just disappeared without a phone call. Only days later when a letter came did I learn that they had spent three days in the air force base ten minutes from home, waiting for a transport to take them to the Dominican Republic. It was a really traumatic time for me, with Dan away, worried about his safety and mine without him. I felt so backward. But I learned quickly to take care of myself and the children. Ignorance was a luxury I couldn't afford.

I never learned when he would be coming back. One day he just appeared, as suddenly as he had gone, exactly the way my father did when I was a little girl, the same age as our son when Dan was gone. When he came home from the Dominican Republic, Dan felt disillusioned with army life, with the half-hearted attempts of the war strategy he had just witnessed, with being called away from us. He mentioned to a friend, almost in passing, that if some other opportunity would come up, he would get out of the army as a career. Then one Sunday not long after that, we were sitting on the couch and the phone rang. It was a long distance call from a small congregation in Illinois, saying that they were looking for a rabbi and had heard he might be available. To me that phone call was a sign from God that Dan should leave the army. I didn't care what job he took, or where, as long as he got out. He went to New York to discuss job possibilities with faculty at the Yeshiva from which he had graduated, as well as other colleagues and his family. Everyone he spoke with discouraged him from looking elsewhere. They said he had such a secure job in the army, with cushy assignments, even if he were sent to a war zone, and a good pension not long off. They told him he'd never make it in the dog-eat-dog world on the outside. I thought that was nonsense, I knew he'd make it, I told him he had to get out, he had to take the risk. I knew we wouldn't starve, and I was afraid for him if he stayed in, and afraid our marriage wouldn't survive another, maybe longer, separation. I knew what went on between the soldiers and the nurses, and I didn't know if I could take the loneliness at home. I never let up, even though I was worried that if he didn't like a different job it would be my fault.

He took a job as a rabbi in a small town in Massachusetts, and turned in his resignation to the army. Even after that, he got a call from Washington pleading with him to go to Saigon, with promises of all the comforts of home. The army needed him desperately, but by then, the decision had been made. It wasn't too long after that a Jewish chaplain flying by helicopter from one base to another was shot down and killed. All along people had said Dan was just a chaplain, not in any danger, but after that incident even my mother-in-law thanked me for getting her son out of the army. I told her just thank God that Dan's alive.

If I thought I was in the limelight as a chaplain's wife, it was nothing in comparison to being in this small town. But they were happy years in Springfield. I assumed my role as president of the Sisterhood, giving convocations, greeting members of the congregation, chairing this and that. Dan and I both enrolled at a nearby university, Dan for his Ph.D., I as an undergraduate. Everyone said it would be impossible to get my credits transferred from Europe, but I found a man who told me how to do it. There's always a way. Springfield was a nice town, we were liked, and I began to feel important for the first time in my life.

School helped me prove to myself that I was worthy of being Dan's wife. But the work was difficult. There was so much I had never been taught about doing; research, footnotes, Mark Twain and all the American literature others had read in high school, that was all new for me. But I enjoyed it, and I knew that when I graduated I wanted to go to work. That was a total shock to Dan. "No wife of mine is going to work!" he said at first. But when he realized how determined I was, he suggested I go to the board of education and tell them I knew French and German, and although I'd never had an education course in my life, they hired me immediately as a substitute teacher. Just as I was getting my B.A. in May, the last six weeks of the public school year, the German teacher left and I took her place. I had no idea what I was doing, but I survived; and they must have thought I had done something right, because the following summer the school board offered me a part-time job, which was just what I wanted with two young children at home. However, they insisted I go back to school to get some education courses, and so I went back for my master's degree in teaching.

As soon as I got my degree, Dan was offered a job in a larger congregation in Oklahoma. It was a terribly difficult year after we moved. Part of it was that I had changed so much, that now I began to demand things from Dan, not just superficial help at home, but a true equality. He seemed to never have time on weekends or at night for the kids or for me, and being in another new town was an additional adjustment. I did some research for Dan for his dissertation and I worked very hard, but I felt unappreciated. I was thrown back into my mother's role of raising the children alone, back into the position of rabbi's wife without a separate identity. I had changed too much to tolerate that, and Dan was totally confused by my discontent. I was nothing like the nineteen-year-old girl he married, dedicated to making him happy. I wasn't at all sure we were going to make it.

I went back to Germany to see my parents. My mother asked me if I'd ever talked to Dan about how I felt, about the cause for my unhappiness, and I realized that I never had. When I came home, we did begin talking, which helped, and I found a full-time teaching job, which made me less demanding of Dan's time. While I was at work, I met another teacher, a man who became my friend, someone I could really talk to. He isn't Jewish; in fact, his grandparents were nobility in Poland, Catholics who owned the Jews. But to this day, twelve years later, he is the kind of person I can rely on. He listened to me, and he respected my ability as a teacher, when I had the feeling Dan didn't think my job was important. He was separate from my husband, from the community in which we lived. I was nobody's wife or mother; I was my own person at school. I built up the foreign language department and became department chairman. When Dan would mention this woman or that, intelligent or good looking, I could finally laugh, after all those years. When he compliments me now about my teaching, it makes me feel good. I know he means it, and I know I deserve it. I love being in the classroom; all of my problems disappear. Even later, if I remember them, I'm able to see them in a different way.

I won't allow myself to be pushed around, and I am learning I don't have to give excuses when I say "no." Other teachers look at me as though I am the Rock of Gibralter. I have come a long way from the child who did whatever I was told. The older I get, the more I think that the people who follow the crowd don't make it. It's just like in the Holocaust, you have to do what your own brain tells you, as my father did. My mother didn't want to leave the ghetto. Her attitude was, "Together we'll live, together we'll die." My father's response was, "Separately we'll live, together we'll die." It's thanks to his not being a follower that my mother and I and many others are alive today. Only in the past six or eight years have I understood my father's contributions to me. I even look like him, and his sister. Growing up I was told I was like my father's mother, which wasn't a compliment at the time because he never got along with her. She was supposedly a very determined, strong woman. It's funny, I never saw myself like that, but perhaps I was until I married Dan, when I felt like a puppy needing Dan's approval. To this day I very seldom do anything against his wishes, although this is one of those times. He really didn't think I should get involved with discussing the Holocaust, but this is something I really wanted to do, that I knew I needed to do for myself. And I think he realizes now that talking to you has been a very helpful experience. It has helped me clarify myself to myself, and to him, too. Until now my reactions have often confused me. No wonder I wasn't understandable to him; it frightened both of us.

Many years ago when they had the first Yom Hashoa commemoration at the Jewish Community Center, somebody had the bright idea to give everyone who came a star of David, a yellow star like they had to wear. It makes me cry now just to remember it. When they wanted to pin that star on me, I started shaking and crying, and I couldn't stop. It's one of the few times in my life I've had no control over myself. I couldn't understand why I was so upset. I don't remember ever wearing a yellow star like that myself or seeing one on my parents. But those times were too traumatic for me to play games about, whatever I've repressed about the details.

I still am afraid of the unknown, of being without, which I'm sure is a result of such an insecure childhood. Last year my son got married. It was a very Orthodox ceremony, and when I saw him in his black coat and top hat, I had this eerie feeling that I had seen this long ago in my far distant past, though I couldn't place it exactly, and I started to cry. But when I was a two-year-old child in Poland in an Orthodox family, this was how my grandfather must have looked, and it was like having him back again, being just where I belonged. . . . Isn't it amazing how history repeats itself?

3
Hedy

Hedy lived in a small town in Germany, unaware that she was Jewish until she entered school and was segregated from the other children. Following her father's return from a forced labor camp, Hedy's parents sent her on a children's transport to England. She supplied me with translations of letters sent her for years by her parents, articles written about her, and artifacts that were relevant to her experiences during the Holocaust. She was always punctual and eager to tell her story.

Hedy is meticulous in her speech and controlled in her affect, a woman-in-charge who expects a great deal from herself and others. Her apartment overlooks a railroad track, so that she can always see who is coming and who is going through her community. Unlike Naomi (see Chapter 5), Hedy speaks of herself as a survivor of the Holocaust. She is acutely aware of the devestation the Holocaust caused her and is committed to making something positive out of these experiences.

There was always music in our house. Even after Hitler came to power and Jews couldn't go to concerts, I was allowed to stay up and to listen to the opera on the radio, though it didn't start until very late at night. I remember hearing La Scala, following along with the libretto next to my parents. On Sundays, Papa and I would go for long walks. He'd start off singing, "Kling klang, sing sang, a fellow goes out into the world." He'd give me an assignment for the week. I was supposed to do research on a topic and the next Sunday we'd discuss it. In the fall or winter when it got dark early, my mother would sit with me on the couch singing old German folk songs. I'd join in when I knew the songs, the night getting darker and darker, the two of us waiting for my father.

My father was very different from the people around him, especially on an intellectual level. Mother came from Hanau, Germany, far from Kippenheim, where my father was from and where we lived. They met at a fair, which I always thought was so romantic. Other people's marriages were arranged within families they knew, but not my parents'. My father's family never accepted my mother, she was always the outsider, just barely tolerated. I grew up realizing that my parents were thought of as strange. Papa must have felt very isolated in our little village, working at a business that didn't really use his creative abilities. He used to sing his song, "A soldier stands on the banks of the Volga, in the darkest night, alone, standing guard for his fatherland."

I didn't know that I was Jewish until I was in the first grade. Our maid, Paula, used to play Santa Claus and take me to church with her. We never celebrated Jewish holidays in our home, though I'd been to synagogue to visit. I felt very uncomfortable in the Jewish homes of friends. Sometimes I wished our home were more like theirs, but when I actually visited at their houses, I couldn't wait to get back to my house where everything was familiar. I never felt like I belonged anywhere.

During my first week of public school, the teacher said, "The next hour will be religious instruction. All the Catholic children, raise your hands." I raised mine, but the teacher knew me and said, "No, you're not Catholic, put your hand down, Hedy." All the Catholic children were sent to one room, and then the teacher asked all the Lutheran children to raise their hands. I raised mine again, but the teacher said I wasn't Lutheran.

"What am I then?" I asked. She said that I was Jewish. I yelled at her that I wasn't and that I was going to tell my mother what she had asked when I got home. But my mother said the teacher was right, that I was Jewish, and so were my parents, grandparents, aunts and uncles, our whole family. "Well, maybe you all are, but not me," I said. And I thought that would finish it.

After four years I transferred to a real gymnasium which I was probably only allowed to attend because my father had been a World War I veteran. There were about a dozen Jewish children in the entire school when I first entered. But by 1938 one boy and I were the only Jewish children left. Many Jewish families had already emigrated from Germany. The days the girls in my class would talk to me were better days, but sometimes they totally ignored me or said nasty things or pushed me. My father talked about the future, sending me to school in France or Switzerland. Maybe he believed the fantasy, but I still had to go to this school each day feeling terribly alone.

Soon after Hitler came to power, my father wrote to some relatives in Chicago asking him to give us an affidavit to get to the United States, but the man wrote back that he was lucky to have a job himself these days, and he was sure if we waited, the situation would get better for us in our own country. "Wait and things will get better!" That advice sticks in my throat whenever someone says that. Things don't always get better. Or maybe they get a heck of a lot worse.

November 9, 1938, was a Wednesday night. After the news on the radio, just before I went to bed, my parents told me if I heard strange noises during the night I should get up immediately and go inside the wardrobe in the hall, but I should not try to get to them. When I asked why, I was told not to ask questions, which was totally contrary to the way I had been raised. Until then, I always questioned and always got answers.

Nothing happened to disturb my sleep that night, and the next morning the sun was shining as I rode my bicycle to school in Ettenheim, five or six miles from my home. As we got close to school, I saw a whole row of broken windows in a building where a Jewish dentist lived and had his office. Somehow I knew those windows had been broken because he was Jewish.

About half an hour after school started the principal, a very mild-mannered, soft-spoken, kind man came to class. He pointed at me and said, "Get out, you dirty Jew." I heard his words, but I couldn't believe what I had heard. I asked him to repeat what he had said. He came over to me, grabbed me by my elbow and pushed me out the door. "Get out, you dirty Jew!" I stood in the hall trying to understand what I had done to make him so angry, afraid that my parents would be angry, too, if I went home from school so early. Kids came out wearing their coats. Some of them pushed me and called me a dirty Jew as they passed. I didn't know what to do, but I went back in the classroom after everyone had gone and sat at my desk and tried to study. After a while this one other Jewish child, Hans Durlacher, wandered into my classroom not knowing what to do either. I continued to pretend to study while he looked out the window. Eventually he yelled to me to come to look.

There were a group of men chained together, four in a row, being marched down the street by SS men in black uniforms with whips. "Schneller, schneller" ("faster, faster") they yelled. We knew the men in chains were Jews. I tried to call home, but our phone was disconnected. My father's business phone, all of the phones of people we knew, "Disconnected," the operator said. I took the back alleys home. Our green shutters, always open during the day, were closed, the front door locked. I rang the bell but nobody answered, even though my mother should have been home at that time. A man walked down the street, a man I knew to be a Nazi, but I ran up to him to ask if he knew where my mother was. "I don't, but if I find the bitch, I'll kill her," he barked at me.

The shortest way to my aunt's house was through the business district. People were breaking windows of a Jewish hardware store, reaching in and stealing things, laughing like it was all a carnival, one big joke. I hoped nobody would recognize me or notice me and I just kept going until I saw my aunt and mother looking out of the second story of my aunt's house. My mother was wearing my aunt's clothes, which were much too big for her. She looked grotesque as she told me how some men had come to our house and had arrested my father. He was still in his pajamas, they didn't even give him time to get dressed before they took him away. The last thing he told her was to try to find me, for us to try to stay together. Then the men broke the windows, slit open our big feather eiderdowns, and my mother ran to my aunt's house in her nightgown.

After I got there, a group of people came out of the village hall. We could see them from our window, as they were marched in chains in various states of undress, whipped by Nazis. Among them we saw my father, and hoped he could see us all together standing in the window. After they marched away, we heard loud banging downstairs at the door. We ran to the attic and hid in an old wardrobe while the banging continued. Then, just as suddenly, it stopped, and there was total silence. I whispered to my mother that I wanted to get out of there. Not just out of the wardrobe, I wanted to get out of Germany.

That night I was too terrified to sleep alone, so the three of us stayed in one bedroom. I wouldn't even go to the bathroom alone. For two weeks we knew nothing of where my father and the other men had been taken. Then a pre-printed postcard arrived from Dachau saying not to send money, not to send packages, not to send pictures or newspapers; only my father's name and address, and our name and address in my father's handwriting. After that, Mother went to the Gestapo office in Karlsruhe to try to get more information. The first time she left me, I was so frightened that now something would happen to her, too, but each day she went and came back, so I began to have faith that she would be all right.

On Monday of the fourth week that my father was gone, the Gestapo office said Papa would be home that week. In fact, that very day other men started arriving home. We went to visit some of them and saw their heads had been completely shaved. By the end of the week, when my father had still not come home, my mother wouldn't even get out of bed. She was thoroughly convinced that Papa was dead.

While we were trying to convince her there was still hope, we heard a knock at our door. Mother wanted us to hide in the attic again, but I ran out of the bedroom to the living room window. There was a man with a hat and coat at the door. Even though his face was hidden, I knew it was my father. "It's Papa," I screamed, but my mother, thinking it was a Nazi, tried to hold me back. I ran downstairs, and when I opened the door and my father took his hat off, I screamed, "My God, they shaved your hair!" I had thought no one would dare to do this to my father. He was different from all the other men in Kippenheim.

When we got Papa inside, we tried to get him to take his coat off, but he said he was too cold, so we put more coals on the stove. But the cold had nothing to do with it. He didn't want us to see how he'd been beaten, how swollen his arms were. Mother had to cut the sleeves open so he could take off his coat. Later that morning while he was shaving, I heard a thump in the bathroom. Papa had had a heart attack. Jewish doctors weren't allowed to treat him, but our old family doctor, a Christian, came that very night to see my father until he recovered.

My father's plans to leave Germany hadn't worked for himself and my mother, but he had discovered a cousin of my grandfather's, Mrs. Simon, who had gone to England as a girl and was by then a lady in her seventies. She agreed to sponsor my going to England. A few Sundays before I was to leave, my father and I took a walk together as we always had. That day he asked me to discuss the immortality of the June bug. I thought this was supposed to be a lesson in sex education, and I didn't want to discuss this topic with him, but he wouldn't let it drop. "Why are the June bugs immortal?" he asked. "Well, before they die they have babies. The babies grow up and have more babies, and that goes on one generation after the other." He seemed satisfied to let the discussion end there.

I was excited to leave Germany, thinking that now I would be going to school in England, just like Papa had always promised. I was fourteen years old, eager to learn English. Only I wasn't eager to leave my bicycle behind. My bike was such a wonderful bike, and I was so proud of it. There were some stamps, too, that I wasn't supposed to take with me, but those I smuggled into my suitcases at the last minute, after the customs official sealed them shut.

As the day got closer for me to leave, I began to have my doubts about why my parents were sending me away. I decided I wasn't their biological child, that I was adopted, and now they simply wanted to get rid of me. My parents had arranged for me to go on a children's transport. There were five hundred children on that train, the youngest were twins six months old, the oldest was sixteen. After I was on the train, I saw my parents run to the end of the platform with tears streaming down their faces as they struggled to suppress them. Thank God I saw that, because then I realized how much they loved me. It was their love that allowed them to send me away. I watched from the window until they got smaller and smaller, until finally they were two little dots and then they were gone. I wrote them a letter that very minute on the train to tell them I understood. I think at that moment I grew up.

I felt very protective of my parents' feelings. I didn't want to worry them about me, so I never wrote to them of any of the horrible things that happened to me. At first we could write to each other directly, but once England and Germany were at war with each other, there were Red Cross messages that came from them. Not many, and they were very brief; twenty-five words including the address. But my parents knew people in France, Holland, Switzerland, and we corresponded by sending our mail through them. My parents didn't write about the details of what was happening to them any more than I told them my troubles. At first they wanted to know all about my life in England, every little detail; whom I was meeting, what I was studying, what I wrote to my other relatives. They worried if more than a few days went by without hearing from me. As time went on, they asked for me to try to help get them out of Germany. I went to the Woburn house, to a rabbi, to anyone I could and asked for help, but I was too young to really know what to do. And I was struggling just to survive myself.

In London I was placed with a family. Mrs. Simon paid for my room and board, but they didn't feed me. I had a piece of toast and tea for breakfast, two pieces of toast and tea for lunch, and two pieces of toast and tea for supper. Sundays I got a cookie as a treat. I guess they made money from the board Mrs. Simon paid, because there was food for the family, just not for me. Mrs. Simon and her daughter left for France two or three days after I arrived in London, and I never had the chance to tell her how bad things were for me. In school I was ashamed not to have candy or cookies to share with the other kids, and when they offered me some of theirs, I simply said I didn't want any, when I was dying to take it.

In July, when Mrs. Simon and her family came back from France, her daughter, Mrs. Mayer, called to see how I was. "Hungry," I said. She invited me to her house, but I had no carfare to get there. That's when I found out I was supposed to be getting an allowance. Mrs. Mayer spoke to the woman of the house and arranged for me to visit a few days later. When I got there, I ate, and I didn't stop all day. Mrs. Mayer didn't want to believe what I told her had been happening, but she could see for herself how much weight I had lost, how my clothes just hung on me as they hadn't when I had arrived. She gave me money for food and said she'd find me a new place to live after school was over that summer.

For the next two years I stayed with another family, the Simmones, who were extremely poor, but probably would have taken food from their own mouths before they'd let me go without. When I turned sixteen, Mrs. Simon explained to me that July would be the last of school for me and that I'd have to get a job. I was flabbergasted to learn this because I hadn't finished high school yet, and I had always planned to go to the university. I had no job skills, but Mrs. Mayer found me a job as a live-in for a cantor. I was to be a companion for his daughter, a girl about my age. She was a strange girl, and my only real responsibility was to be her friend. For this I got a roof over my head, food, and an allowance. I thought I was on my way to becoming a millionaire.

It was 1940. The heavy air raids started in London, and a shelter was built in the garage of the cantor's house, with five bunks in it, though there were only four of us living there at the time; a man who was the cantor's friend, the daughter, the cantor and me. I thought the extra bunk must be for the child's mother, who would be coming home, but that wasn't what the cantor had in mind. He had a lady friend who joined us once we moved into the shelter. One night I woke up to this commotion in the single bunk. There was a candle lit by his bed, but I knew I wasn't supposed to see what was going on. It frightened me, all the noise and commotion. Soon the noise subsided and I went back to sleep. In the morning the little girl asked if I had heard anything during the night, but I pretended not to know what she was talking about. Every night this happened, and I became increasingly frightened until finally I called Mrs. Mayer again and told her I had to leave the cantor's house. She didn't question me, she just told me to pack my bags, not to explain anything to anyone, that she would take care of everything.

She found me a place in a girls' home for refugees. The matron who ran it exploited all of us. There were three separate buildings to this institution, and the one I lived in never had heat or hot water. Once a week, for an hour, those of us from my building were allowed to bathe in the matron's building, which did have heat. But because of my work hours, often I missed my turn. My body was filthy, crusty, and my clothes were gray since I couldn't do laundry either. Whatever money we made we were supposed to hand over to the matron.

Very shortly after I moved there, the girl in the next bed had malaria. She should have been hospitalized, because she was so sick she couldn't get out of bed. But the staff nurse said she was just lazy. We used to steal food from the dining hall to bring back to her, but one night she died, lying in the bed next to me. Compared to her, the rest of us felt lucky. We all suffered together, waiting to be reunited with our families. It never occurred to me that I wouldn't be going back to Kippenheim, or that I wouldn't see my parents again.

I continued to hear from home fairly regularly until I got a letter from my parents in November of 1940 which read, "As you will note at the top of the letter, we have changed our address." The letter had been sent from Camp de Gurs in the foothills of the Pyrenean Mountains. This was all they said, and I had no idea what this meant, although I wasn't too worried about it. I continued to hear off and on from them until 1941, when my father wrote that he'd requested to be transferred to a camp near Marseilles because he wanted to register with the American consulate there. On the twelfth of August, 1942, he wrote saying, "I'm going to be deported to an unknown destination. It may be a very long time before you hear from me, but I will try to stay in touch. Don't worry about me."

On the first of September, my mother wrote, "The last few weeks have been very difficult for us. The last letter from your father was on the twelfth of August. A lot of people have been sent, and tomorrow is my turn. It may be a very long time before you'll hear from me again. You must be brave, carry your head high and be good. I hope to meet your father somewhere because then we can carry our lot together." It was the first time she ever complained to me. After that, there was one more postcard from her, postmarked the fourth of September, 1942. She must have known something. She was on her way to Drancy, and she mailed the card in Montauban, immediately north of her camp. She said, "Traveling to the East and sending you these final good-bye greetings from Montauban." And then she signed her name.

After that, every day I ran home to look for mail from my parents, but it never came. They had written that it might be a long time before I'd hear. How long is a long time? A month? A year? Maybe not today, but maybe tomorrow or next week. Since the other girls in the home had lost contact with their parents too, it didn't seem so unnatural not hearing from mine. I wanted to be able to share things with them, to tell them at least the good parts of my days. But there was no place to write.

In the building next to our girls' home lived men who were refugees from the Spanish Civil War. A lot of the girls went back and forth to their building or went to dances hoping to pick up men. I felt very critical of this. Maybe part of my discomfort was that I wasn't as pretty as the other girls or didn't have the clothes they did. Maybe I worried a little that I wouldn't be accepted.

Instead, I spent my time across the street with an organization called the Free German Youth, a political organization of German Jewish refugees whose goal it was to go back to Germany after the war and reeducate the Germans. The girls in the home were just as critical of my activities as I was of theirs. But I really enjoyed the people in the Free German Youth organization. They helped establish a strong political conscience in me which remains important to this day. Besides, I thought I was different from the other girls in the home. None of them read or thought much about what had happened to us. I took classes at a college nearby, not for a degree, just to learn about psychology, for example. I cared about concerts and literature, not just dancing, or how tall the men I dated were. As in Germany, I found myself to be different from the people around me, not in the mainstream. I think, too, I had been programmed from a very young age to think of myself as different, to keep myself apart.

Because of the despair of the women, there was an awful lot of stealing in the home, stealing of things that had no monetary value. The girl in the next bed had her parents' pictures stolen. One day when I came up to our room, one of the girls, who was extremely ugly, was dancing around the bed completely naked except for a big bow around her waist singing, "I'm so pretty." It was really painful to me to see these basically decent human beings driven to such strange acts, and I was terribly uncomfortable being surrounded by them.

Mrs. Simon and Mrs. Mayer had moved away from London without letting me know where they had gone. I didn't have anywhere else to go. I worked for the matron in her doll factory to pay for food and lodging, then I worked at Harrods' department store, making children's clothes. After a year or so, I began to think I should be doing something more important, more patriotic than making clothes for pampered children with a war going on. I got a new job in a factory making parts for the war effort until a machine malfunctioned and crushed one of my fingers.

By this time a friend and I had moved to our own apartment. When my finger healed, I changed jobs to work in a bullet factory. A bizarre thing happened to me working there. The machine I operated had to function twenty-four hours a day without ever shutting down. If I needed to take a break, I had to call the supervisor to find a replacement so the machine would keep functioning. I don't know what made me do it, but once I left the machine without calling to anyone first, without really knowing why I walked away. Just at that moment, the glass blocks overhead came crashing down from the skylight onto my machine. It was the time of the V2s which traveled faster than sound. One of them had exploded, and the pressure had shattered the glass. Had I stayed at the machine, I probably would have been killed. It was spooky, like something saved me.

When the war ended, I went back to Germany as I had planned, intending to help reeducate the Germans. I was fortunate to get a job working for the American government censoring German mail in an attempt to find out information about Nazis. I never really thought about what feelings I would have going back to my country, other than the hope of going back to Kippenheim to find my parents. But as the train pulled across the border and stopped, children came onto the platform, begging. Other people with me were giving them candy and gum, but suddenly those children in front of me weren't children I was seeing, but little Nazis, and I hated them. For weeks as the begging continued wherever we went, I refused to give them anything. Eventually, I was able to think that these children were too young to have done anything, even to have known what had gone on, and I was able to give them candy too. But they had to eat it in front of me so I could be sure no one else, no one older, could get what I was handing out. After a few months, I realized that I was too full of anger and hate to carry out my plan to reeducate the German people, and I realized I couldn't stay permanently in Germany.

The decision to leave Germany also meant cutting off a serious romantic relationship that had started back in London. My fiancé was committed to moving back to Germany and was planning to meet me there some months later. But once I faced the fact that I couldn't make Germany my home, I wrote to him that I'd found someone else, although this was not the truth. I didn't give him the chance to choose between living in Germany or living with me elsewhere; I made the decision for him. Maybe I couldn't stand the thought that he might choose Germany over me.

It was still impossible for me to believe what had happened during the war. I had certainly heard stories, and I had visited a displaced persons' camp where some still wore prisoners' uniforms. I had helped organize trucks to bring packages to the people living there, but the behavior of the Jews in those camps was terribly disturbing to me. I saw, not once, but many, many times, Jews attacking Germans, taking things from them, cameras, rings, watches. They had been treated like animals in the camps, and now they treated the Germans this way. It made me so upset to see this, I stopped working in the DP camp.

I knew before I left Germany I had to go back to Kippenheim to look for my parents, but I was afraid to go, afraid to let go of the hope that they would be there waiting. Twice I got on the train for home, and twice I turned around. But finally I couldn't avoid it any longer. The train station in Kippenheim is about half an hour's walk from the village. It was a walk I had taken many times with my parents, and as I went back I recognized every stone along the way. But as I approached the first house in Kippenheim, suddenly I became terrified, as though it were 1938 again, and everyone living there was a Nazi. I walked straight ahead, not daring to look as I passed my own house. I decided to go to the village hall and ask the mayor for help.

The mayor said he would go with me to my house, and on the way he explained that our home had been divided into efficiency apartments. He knew some of the families living there and would ask them to let us in. When we got there, the outside of the building had holes in it from bullets, the shutters hadn't been painted, the street had been widened so part of the front yard was gone, and the big tree that had been on the side of the house was no longer there. When I saw this, I didn't want to go inside any more. I wanted to remember my house the way it had been, with things inside that were still ours. I had also planned to go to the cemetery in Schmieheim where I have family buried, but this I completely forgot to do. It was as though I were still a little girl, and my mother was still telling me a cemetery was not a place for me to be.

I ended up extending my stay in Germany because I got a job with the American government at the Nuremberg trials as a research analyst, looking for evidence against the Nazis. I was assigned specifically to the trial of the German doctors who performed medical experiments at the camps. When I saw the documents in preparation for the trials, I learned the truth for myself. The atrocities the Jews had been through were right there in the photographs, the documents. After reading the descriptions of the experiments performed on the prisoners and how they had suffered, I wasn't able to eat without vomiting. Some of the survivors told their stories at the trial. One young man who testified had just become aware of having been sterilized. Another young woman had had the fleshy part of her leg cut open with rusty nails and pieces of wood implanted in it to see what would happen to her. She was carried into the trial by two GIs since she could no longer walk. I couldn't sleep at night after listening.

I sat in on Göring's trial as well. Because I worked at Nuremberg, I had more freedom to move around than other visitors. During one recess, the defendants remained in the dock, and I went over and stood directly in front of Göring, just staring at him. I could see he was becoming uncomfortable, and he asked his German defense counsel, "Who is this little one?" His attorney said he didn't know, but they'd better say nothing and let me stay there. I continued to stand in front of him, little Hedy Wachenheimer from Kippenheim, making Göring squirm. The more I saw and heard at the trials, the more I became emotionally overloaded. I put a wall between what I had to do and my feelings. My body continued, but the rest of me I put away.

During this period, I lived in a small apartment with a coworker. We were assigned a German maid about our age, and the maid and I became friends. My roommate couldn't understand my being friendly with a lowly servant, but I looked at this young woman as my equal. She appreciated literature and cultural activities, but because of circumstances, she was cleaning my apartment. I believed her when she said her parents had been anti-Nazis.

As my work on the trials came to an end, I began to make plans for getting to the United States. My mother's two brothers had come to this country in 1938. They had planned to send for my parents, but that became impossible. In the summer of 1947, I asked them to give me an affidavit to come to the U.S., which they did. But I found that getting here was still extremely complicated. In order to emigrate, I had to return to England to get a quota number. I was told it would be a year's wait for getting passage on a ship to America. I knew if my quota number came up, I had to take advantage of it or I'd miss my opportunity to leave, so I got a job in a travel agency with an employer who promised to get me passage on a ship if I would buy him nylons for his girlfriend and American cigarettes at the PX. I had no feelings about leaving Germany; I was too busy taking care of arrangements.

In May 1948 I boarded the *Queen Elizabeth*. There was never a cloud in the sky during the five-day trip. I spent most of the time on the deck getting a tan like I've never had before or since. My Aunt Elese was at the pier waiting for me. She hadn't seen me since I was thirteen years old. Here I was, all grown up, wearing my new mustard-colored suit, and she looked right past me until I said, ''I'm Hedy.''

My aunt and uncle had a room waiting for me at their house. They wanted me to do whatever I wanted to do, but not to work. They inundated me with presents and wanted to take care of me, to be the child they had never had. But I was uncomfortable having them wait on me. I had been on my own so long, I was drowning in all their care and love. I decided to move out and find myself a job. They weren't happy about this, but eventually my aunt helped me find an apartment, and we had an excellent relationship after that.

For the next several years, all of the jobs I had were working with immigrants. Unconsciously, I think I chose these positions so I could continue to look for my parents. By 1950 my circle of acquaintances was still all European. I wanted an American experience and decided to move away from New York. I took out a map of the United States, closed my eyes and let my finger drop. That was how I made the move to Minneapolis.

In August of 1952, I married. I thought for the first five months that Felix and I were happy. Then one night in January, we went to his parents' home for dinner. As we got back to our apartment, the phone was ringing.

It was Felix's mother calling to say that his father had died of a heart attack. We went back to his parents' house and agreed to stay with his mother, for what I thought would be just a few nights. The first night I slept in what had been Felix's room, and Felix stayed with his mother in her room. I didn't find this strange, considering the shock she had been through. But Felix never moved out of his mother's bedroom, which had only one bed in it. In April, after three months of living this way, I moved back to our apartment alone. The following Monday, I was served with divorce papers which had been drawn up two months before, secretly.

I was devastated by the divorce. Even as I thought back on the early months of our marriage, there had been no indication that Felix had been unhappy or that there was anything unnatural about his relationship with his mother. I had thought it was a warm, loving relationship, but normal. Strangely, it had been his mother who had encouraged me to enroll in college. I had tried once before, but the New York Board of Regents had told me I had to start back in the third grade if I wanted to continue my education. Once my marriage ended, I tried again. The University of Minnesota gave me a placement test and determined I could enter their university immediately.

Those were hectic years after the divorce, between earning money and studying. By now I was thirty years old. I had friends who wanted me to meet a man they knew, but I was afraid of getting involved in another relationship, the way my first marriage had worked out. I was convinced there was some deficiency in me. But one night the phone rang, and it was Arnie; my friends had given him my number. We talked from 11:30 until 2:00 in the morning. Something just clicked between us. Shortly after we began dating, Arnie moved to a new job in New Jersey. We corresponded until school was over for me in June, and I went to visit him. I agreed to move to New Jersey after that.

Arnie had warned me that his parents were strange. One Sunday we went to meet them. As soon as I walked in the door, I was instructed to sit down. His mother handed me a Hebrew prayer book and told me to read. She wanted proof that I was Jewish. I should have been aware from this beginning that Arnie's mother and I weren't going to get along and that Arnie and I would have our problems because of her, but I didn't want to see this.

We married in November of 1955. Very soon after, the one time we didn't use birth control, I became pregnant. Five minutes after we had had intercourse, I told Arnie I could feel something bubbling inside me. I could feel the cells dividing. Of course, he didn't believe me. Even when the doctors said that I was pregnant, we didn't tell Arnie's parents. I think he was ashamed for them to know that we were having sex, even though we were married. When I was five and a half months pregnant and showing, Arnie finally believed that maybe we were going to have a baby; he still hoped his parents wouldn't notice.

Once Howard was born, Arnie was thrilled, but he was afraid of the baby. When I came home from the hospital, there was a huge physics book under the crib. Arnie said he wanted Howard to absorb the knowledge in it. The book stayed under the baby's bed for a good two or three months. When Arnie needed the book himself, he'd lie on the floor under the crib and read it.

The relationship with Arnie's parents got progressively worse. His mother was so weird. She never bathed when she came to visit or changed her clothes, even when the baby peed on her dres. Once she told her son that he should never have married me, that German Jews were all alike, and that it was too bad the same thing that had happened to my parents hadn't happened to me too. I lashed back at her, and later Arnie wanted me to forget what she had said and apologize. But I wouldn't, and I never visited in her home after that, although Arnie went and took our son to spend time with his parents.

When Howard was four years old, I became pregnant with our second child. Arnie was very angry about this because his company was planning to move to St. Louis, and Arnie thought it was terrible timing. When I was three months pregnant, my water bag broke. I became dehydrated and had to have transfusions every day. I went from 110 pounds to 93 pounds and was so sick I begged the doctor to abort the baby. He said he couldn't do that but that I'd never carry to term. I took that as a challenge and wanted to defy the doctor. Then I wanted the baby more than ever. I became almost totally useless those next few months. I hemorrhaged all the time and couldn't cook or look after Howard. Arnie kept saying, "Women are pregnant all the time, have been for thousands of years without trouble. Why are you so different?" as though I could control it. He was concerned about having his shirts ironed, about having me available to be supportive of him. I was ruining all of his plans.

When the baby came, it was premature, and the doctor put me out with gas for the delivery. When I woke up and saw Arnie's face, I knew something terrible had happened. Arnie told me our baby was dead, and both of us cried. An autopsy had already been done, so I never saw the baby. The rabbi advised me against having a funeral for Eric and said that I would regret it if I did. But I wouldn't hear of this. As a child, when my grandmother died, I wasn't at her funeral, and there was no funeral for my parents. It was as if they all had gone up in smoke. Our baby lived twelve hours, he had a name, and he was going to have a burial, no matter what rabbi disapproved. The day I went home from the hospital, I went to the cemetery to see for myself that Eric Marc Epstein had a grave, a place that I could visit.

It took me a long time to get over the baby's death. In the meantime, we moved to St. Louis and left behind the support of people we knew. I felt really isolated, as though we had been deported. Arnie seemed almost relieved there was no baby to interfere with his new job. As time went on, I realized that at some point I was going to get out of this marriage. My goal was to wait until Howard was eighteen.

I began to feel so miniscule that I thought people on the street would walk straight through me, they didn't even know I was there. I felt nonexistent. I became involved with the husband of a friend of mine. At least one person thought I was something. But I realized I was using the man just to feel better about myself, so I ended the relationship.

I wanted to work full-time at a meaningful job, but this threatened Arnie. He didn't want people to think he couldn't support me. He said no one would hire me because I had no skills. "Besides," he said, "you never finish anything you start. You never even finished the relationship with your parents!" One night Arnie awakened me from a dream I was having. I had been screaming "No! No! It's not my fault!" When he awakened me, I realized that the dream was the same one that had recurred twice weekly for years, ever since I'd come to this country. But until this night, I could never remember any of the details. Now I knew what I had been dreaming. I was standing on the ramp of a railway station; my parents were on a train headed for a concentration camp. As the train pulled away, I watched them get smaller and smaller until they were two dots and then disappeared. In the dream I was responsible for sending them away, for killing them. It was my guilt over surviving that was the cause of that dream. After it became clear, the dream only occurred one other time, many years later.

It was a sheer lucky fluke that I got a job at Freedom of Residence. I was on the board when their grant came through, and they were looking to hire staff. Arnie said I was like a cat—if you dropped me from the twelfth floor, I'd land on my feet. He demeaned the job and made no exceptions to his demands on me as a housewife. I decided to deposit my money in my own account and began to prepare for leaving. Arnie resisted, but I was determined to get a divorce. The morning when he finally moved out, I was really scared, even though I had wanted this. I was terribly depressed, but Howard was there and very sensitive to me. Eventually, the house that I had wanted to run away from I enjoyed being in. I enrolled in school and finished first my bachelor's degree, then my master's. Arnie continued to belittle me at every opportunity, even long-distance from Washington where he had moved, blaming me for Howard's lack of interest in science,

Arnie's field. He said it was my fault Howard became engaged to be married before he had even graduated from college. But by then, Arnie couldn't upset me anymore. I had finally turned the corner.

While I was in Washington on business, Arnie became ill and was hospitalized. They diagnosed him as having cancer. I went to visit him in the hospital and offered to have him come back to St. Louis to stay with me. He was too ill to take care of himself, and he was dying. I didn't know if he had anyplace else to go. As soon as he was able to travel, Howard, Terry (Howard's fiancée), and I brought Arnie to St. Louis. He was so sick, the trip was a nightmare, and trying to get him up the stairs to my apartment was worse.

For a short time, he seemed genuinely contented to be there, but then the arguing started, and his anger. A nurse stayed with him during the day while I worked. The week before he died, I fixed dinner and helped him to the table. He lifted up his gown and started to fondle himself in front of me. "Arnie, that's not necessary," I said. With that, he urinated in my plate.

"You've been hypersensitive all your life, and now I'm going to teach you something you'll remember, Hedy. Sit down and eat this." This was our last conversation. I threw the plate into the trash, along with any feelings I had ever had for him, though I continued to care for his body, taking turns with Howard during the night. Howard and I were asleep in the next room when Arnie died. I didn't see it happen; even then death eluded me. I think this had been my reason for having him come home with me, the thought that I might be able to deal with death and dying better if I could actually see it occur. After Arnie died, one more time the old dream came back about my parents on the train going to a concentration camp. But this time I was able to wake myself up and interrupt it. I knew this time the dream had to do with Arnie's death, and I told myself, "No, you are not responsible for this one either." Even after all those years, I still had trouble accepting my parents' death. There was never any documentation to prove that they had died, no gravestone, nothing. When I had tried to talk to Arnie about this, he had simply told me to forget those times. They were over and done with.

In 1980 I went on a pilgrimage to Europe, to the camps where my parents had been taken. I began in France with Camp de Gurs. Something happened to me there, a mystical experience almost, which I have never been able to explain. As I was walking away from the camp, feeling an extraordinary sadness, a stone lying on the ground seemed to me to say "Pick me up, take me with you." I was planning to go to the first international gathering of Holocaust survivors in Israel, and we had been encouraged to bring stones for the construction of a monument to those who had not survived. I picked up the stone and wiped it off. It was a pretty stone, and I put it in my pocket, intending to take it with me to Israel. Weeks later when I was back in the United States, someone pointed out to me that there's a Mogen David on that stone. I took it to a geologist who said the design is nature made.

It was so hard to comprehend, Auschwitz, Birkenau, and especially this quaint little beautiful town named Dachau where my train ended. I found a marker where my father's barrack had been, barrack number 20. I walked all around touching it. When I stood in the middle of the camp and looked off in the distance where the horizon met the earth, the camp went beyond even that. Standing on the ramp where the decisions had been made as to who would live, who would die, suddenly I knew my parents did not survive. As I walked away, I realized that I was humming. "A soldier stands at the banks of the Volga. In darkest night alone standing guard for our fatherland."

I have been told often by other survivors that I am not a survivor because I myself was never in a concentration camp, because I didn't suffer like others did. But I call myself a survivor, and I will go on calling myself that whether they think I'm entitled to the word or not. I know what happened to me and what might have happened. Just a few months ago, the international tracing service sent me my father's prisoner number in Dachau and my mother's transport number from Camp de Rivesaltes to Drancy. There's this giant puzzle I'll never be able to piece together, a question mark about what really happened to my parents. But I have to keep looking for information. "Don't ever forget us," Mother said. I know how important it is that we remember, that we tell the story of the Holocaust over and over again, just as we talk about the Exodus from Egypt each Passover.

When I came to this country, the first woman who trained me for a job in New York was a black woman. At lunchtime she would tell me where I could eat, and I would invite her to go with me, but she always refused. I remember the shock I felt discovering that restaurants wouldn't serve black people. I had thought all that had ended in this country when Lincoln freed the slaves. It was like seeing the signs back in Germany all over again, "Entry forbidden for Jews." I thought, "I've come away to this again." It was the beginning of my involvement in the Civil Rights movement, my life as a political activist in the United States.

There have been other causes since that I have been part of: the Rosenberg trial, fair housing and environment issues, always I have associated myself with minority group rights and efforts toward peace in the world. I was against the Vietnam War before it became a movement. I have worked for redevelopment opportunities for women and now work in a law office with 90 percent of our cases concerning civil rights. I have picketed, marched, written letters, sent telegrams, even been arrested once as a protester against our government's injustices. The sanctuary movement is one to which I am deeply committed. It seems a natural cause for Holocaust survivors, giving refuge to those persecuted by their governments. If more people would have given sanctuary to Jews during Hitler's reign, more would have survived. Some people say they will join the sanctuary movement when it becomes legal. But that does not matter to me. It wasn't legal for righteous Gentiles to hide Jews; they took risks outside the law as we must now for other people who need our protection.

I am terribly pained when I see the Jewish community having a narrow scope to its activities, looking only inward. We must be concerned with people whether they are or are not Jewish, if we want peace in this world. We must sit with the enemy and talk, we must move beyond our own fear and anger over what happened to us during the Holocaust and channel our energies to fight for all oppressed people everywhere.

My political views have been unpopular with a lot of people around me. It took me seven years to obtain citizenship because of my past connection with the Free German Youth and my fiancé in London who became part of the Communist party when he moved back to Germany. Often I express views that make others uncomfortable. But they will not get rid of me. I will continue to be present where I think I need to be and will raise whatever points I think are necessary. Since 1982 I have found a political home within the New Jewish Agenda. This past month I received the Unsung Heroine Award from that organization at a dinner in California. Six of us were selected to be honored. The certificates we each received reads "Thank you for your deep and lifelong commitment to Tikkun Olam, the just re-ordering of the world." I have tried to make something positive out of my experiences in the Holocaust. Because I remember, I must speak out, I must take action. It is a healing process for me, knowing that I have a way to give to others the kind of help that was given to me. Without it, I would not have survived.

4
Regina

Regina is a lovely, well-groomed woman in her fifties. In spite of slow speech and an unsteady walk caused by multiple sclerosis, she has an air of dignity and strength. Before our work together, she had been reluctant to tell her story, saying, "I might commit suicide if I told you what really went on." Almost a year after our initial interview, she decided to participate in this project. She recounted the details of her experiences clearly and in an orderly sequence, without any hint of self-pity.

Regina was born in Radom, Poland, and survived the war in a series of concentration camps, using her initiative to save herself and her brother. Her brother's continual struggle with mental illness has been an overriding worry to Regina. Because he was so young when the war started, without the benefit of the secure years Regina experienced, and because of devastating invasive medical experiments he suffered in Auschwitz, her brother's potential has been severely limited. Regina feels responsible for him, her only remaining family member. As a child in Auschwitz, Regina kept him alive by bringing him soup, and he in turn saved both of them by deciding to hide in Borno when everyone else was taken away. Presently, however, Regina's brother does not correspond with her or return her phone calls or seem willing to acknowledge her existence. She does not want to accept the death of their relationship and is struggling to find some way to reach him.

In Auschwitz, the opportunity to work was lifesaving. Regina still sees hard work as life's only salvation. She has never allowed herself a

*time of letting down, of falling apart. "What good would it do to cry?" she
asked. Yet her eyes tear frequently, as though she is constantly crying over
a hidden sadness, a sadness to which she does not give way. Her body
seems to rebel against the need for so much control. Her story reveals the
strength and determination that guided her through her early years in
America and present life. With the authority of a survivor, she says proudly
of herself, "I have always been a fighter."*

I was born in Radom, Poland, June sixth, 1931. I had then a brother
four years younger than myself, a mother, and a father. All of the memories I have of my early years are so great. My father had two shoe factories,
and we were very well off. I didn't want for anything. On my sixth
birthday, I was given a beautiful bike. It was like a Cadillac. On my
seventh birthday, I was given a beautiful black mahogany piano. We had a
summer cottage, too, where my mother and brother and I would stay all
week in the hot months while my father went back home to work, but he'd
join us on the weekends. When he'd leave again, my brother and I would
stand by the train outside his open window, and he would throw out toys to
us to make sure we would remember him during the rest of the week.

My mother had help in the house, very responsible people she could
leave with my brother and me when she went out with my father. In the
mornings, I was walked to school by a woman in a white hat and dress and
apron, and she wore a cross. I thought she was a nun; I don't know what
she was. She would take off my boots, leave, and come back for me in the
evening. It was a Jewish private school, and we wore navy blue skirts,
white blouses with sailor collars with a white skirt for summer. So prim
and proper. There was never any need for me to take risks.

Family life was extremely important. It was very different from the
life in America today. My parents told me what to do, and I did it. There
was an openness between myself and my parents. In the evenings at dinner
time, we had long discussions about our days, and I was encouraged to
express my ideas. I always knew I had uncles and aunts who loved me. I
was part of something; there was a meaning to life. No one has ever taken
away the emotional security of having had loving parents. Sometimes in
America, when children move away, they forget they have a family.

I still think my father was one of the smartest people I have ever
come across. Hitler came to power [in Poland] in 1939, when I was eight
years old. When the war started in 1939 and the bombs were falling, my
father rented a truck, took my mother, brother, and me, and was going to
drive us to another city. But as we drove farther out of town and saw fires

all around us, he realized that whatever was going on in Radom was happening everywhere, so he changed plans and turned back.

It's surprising what a shock human beings can take and make the best of. When our house was liquidated, we moved into the ghetto with my aunt and uncle. Each of our two families had one bedroom of an apartment and shared the kitchen. I had to stop going to school, but my parents sent me to a lady who knew Hebrew well enough to teach my brother and me. Until this I had only spoken Polish. When my mother and father spoke between themselves and didn't want us to understand, they sometimes spoke Yiddish, but language hadn't mattered to me; Yiddish, Polish, it had all seemed the same before.

The Nazis gave my mother a job sorting clothes, and my father worked with shoes. In spite of my age, they gave me a job putting glue on envelopes. I was one of the youngest children working. My parents explained how lucky it was that I could be useful. Otherwise, I would have been sent to Treblinka like my two aunts and grandmother. Some Jews had escaped from Treblinka and had come back to the ghetto. They had told us there was no life at Treblinka, only death. This is all we knew about the fate of the Jews. My brother was too little to work, and he would have been sent away too, but my parents kept him in the apartment so he wouldn't be noticed. They had different work shifts, so someone was always with him.

Because my father still had money, he was able to pay Jewish kapos to tell him when they were going to take people out of the ghetto to send them away to the camps. Then my father would contact Poles living on the outside and pay them to take my brother and me to their houses to stay until the danger cleared and we could come back to be with our parents. Each time, the night before we had to leave, our parents would sit down and explain to us that Dad was fortunate enough to have the money to send us away, that it was necessary for us to go in order to save our lives, and we were to go with these people and be good kids. Then when it was time, we crawled through the basement windows under the wires surrounding the buildings to the street outside the ghetto where somebody would be waiting for us. We trusted our parents very much.

One time while my brother and I were being kept in hiding in the countryside, we were sitting eating supper and some neighbors came in. "Are these your cousins here?" they asked the Polish farmers, pointing to my brother and me. "Yes," the woman said. But the neighbors didn't believe her. "I don't know what it is. The girl resembles you, but the boy has such a long nose. He looks like a Jew." After that we weren't allowed to be with the family; we were put in the attic for three days. Another time we were sent into hiding, my mother went with us. My father had been taken to work in a shop outside of the ghetto. Someone he worked with kept us with his family for a week. But the woman demanded so much of my mother, my mother knew she resented having us there and was afraid that the woman would turn us in, so she sent a message to my father that he should give some of our jewelry, in addition to the money, to make sure she kept her mouth shut.

When they liquidated the ghetto in Radom, we had to leave our beautiful piano. Once we got to Piunke, we were separated from my father. My mother and my brother and I were given a small room with two bunkers. My mother slept on the top, my brother and me on the bottom. I had a job again, working with bullets in an ammunitions factory. I was maybe ten years old. Most of the others working with me were nineteen or twenty, except for Nancy. We were the only two Jewish girls there. I don't know how it happened, but one day we overslept. When we showed up late for work, we were taken into the office of the Gestapo. The officer said not to let it happen again, and to teach us that he meant it, he took our two heads and knocked them together so hard that I couldn't see afterwards for an hour. He said because of what we had done we had to work twenty-four hours round the clock. But we were lucky; we knew what could have happened to us. At the bus stop in Piunke, sometimes people who had broken the rules were hung, their bodies put up at the bus stop as examples for the rest of us to see. We were always aware when we woke up in the morning today is going to be the end of somebody's life. It was a terrible time; everybody was so scared. There was no happiness, just bitterness. All we were faced with was death. There was no way anybody could protect me anymore.

The numbers of us who made it out of Piunke were few, only the strongest of us, except for my brother, whom we had kept very much hidden. When they liquidated Piunke, my mother and father, brother, and I were put on the train together. But then my father was taken away from us, put on another train and sent to a working camp. As my father was separated from us, I saw a small child taken by its legs, its brains knocked out of it by an SS officer. That was the start of our knowledge of Auschwitz. My mother, brother, and I followed where we were told to go, took off all our clothes and had our heads shaved. We were told that if they shaved our hair, it meant we weren't going to the gas chambers. When you are told that, hair doesn't mean that much to you; it can grow back. We came out of the showers. We were still alive. They gave us wooden shoes, striped shirts and pants. That was in Birkenau.

The ovens were going round the clock. Every day they took out more people. One day they called us up to get a number, a tattoo on our arms. My arms were bleeding from the needles, but on the other hand, we thought, if they bothered giving us a number, they were going to keep us alive. My cousins, my brother, we were all given numbers. But soon my cousins were taken away, and my brother too. We knew it was the end of him. Then my mother was taken away, and I was left on the block by myself. But I wanted to live. I knew I was too young and too little to be taken out of Auschwitz to work, so I used to take cement blocks and hide them in the last row of prisoners when they had a roll call. Then I would stand on them to make myself taller so the SS couldn't see how young I was, so they wouldn't take me to the gas chamber. I saved my life this way for a couple of months.

I'm a fighter. Life is so dear. When you are young, no matter what, you want to live. But when I was discovered standing on those blocks to make myself taller, I don't know what happened to me. I lost consciousness. When I woke up, I was in the hospital. At the time, I didn't know it was Mengele's hospital. I stood up, and I saw that everything around me was dead people. I went through the rows and saw my brother lying there in a bed. I didn't believe it. My mother and I had thought he was dead, that we'd never see him again. We had cried on each other's shoulders about him. And here I passed by and found him in this hospital. He had lost his hair already and all his nails. He was just bone and skin, his arms completely covered with bruises from the injections they had given him. He could hardly cry anymore from pain; there was nothing left of him. He recognized me, though. He knew he was dying slowly, and he couldn't believe I was there. We hugged, thinking he only had hours to live.

I was thirteen years old by then, and I begged for a job in the hospital. They gave me the job of carrying buckets of soup from the kitchen to the patients. There was always a lot left because so many of the sick people died each day, so I took the extra to my brother. One day while I was carrying the bucket outside from the kitchen, I saw my mother in the yard. Until this moment, I thought she had been taken from the camp, but she had been removed to a different part. When I saw her, we yelled and we waved, and I told her I had seen my brother, that he was still alive. I was so glad to tell her, even though I couldn't go to her. That was the last time I saw my mother.

For three or four months I gave my brother the soup. I slept on the floor by him in the hospital. Experiments were going on. God, I could hear the people screaming. When the prisoners came out of the operating room, the blood was all over their bodies. God . . . then in 24 hours they would die. The doctors continued to experiment on my brother by giving him injections, by cutting him. They wanted to see how long he could survive and withstand the pain. They would open up a human body and not close it again so they could watch the healing process. They used to cut tongues off, fingers off. They wanted to see if my brother would go crazy from the injections, to see what stages he would go through first.

My brother and I both got stronger. Then, I can't remember how we got there, but the next thing I knew we were in a camp where I was not surrounded by the white beds, by killings or experiments. It was a children's camp. All of the children there were brothers and sisters or twins. We were at this camp for about a month. My brother started walking. It was like a miracle. Then they told us they needed blood for the soldiers, and it was to come from the children in this camp. Every day a bus came to take the children; every evening it would bring them back on cots, sucking on oranges. The next day the same children would be taken. Within 48 or 62 hours those children died. So it was like a liquidation. Life had so little meaning. You wanted to survive, but yet you knew you weren't going to. Tomorrow would be your day if they didn't take you today. I did not have any hope for us anymore. Finally, they came to get all of the children left and take them out of Borno. But my brother said we shouldn't leave with the others, that we would die if we left with them. We hid in a ditch while the trucks took all the others away. Even then we were afraid to come out, but eventually we did. We wandered into another part of the camp, looking for something to eat, and we discovered some men who were also Polish Jews who had hidden and stayed behind. We went into the basement with these men where they had a hiding place behind cement blocks. They said it wouldn't be long before the Russians would be coming.

But something happened before we were liberated that I have never spoken about until just recently, something that made me so angry I didn't even want to think about it. My brother and I were in that basement with these Jewish men. One of them waited until he had the opportunity to find me alone, and he tried to rape me. I couldn't scream because I didn't know if the Germans were all gone, and I was afraid they would hear me and come and kill us all. But I bit that man so hard he was bleeding, and he couldn't go on with it. I was only thirteen years old. I didn't know about sex or rape, but he was like an animal. This is how he attacked me, and I responded with my own animal instinct. After this, we continued to live in hiding, all of us together. I saw him day in and day out. He did not apologize to me; he thought he had the right to do what he wanted. He's dead now, but I have never forgiven him for what he has done. The thought of being raped, of having my body invaded, is worse to me than death. This is why I have not spoken about it for so long.

Life in the camp turned some people into animals. Our block officer, a Czechoslovakian Jew, was not told to go out and beat us to death like she did. She killed her father and mother to get the job. But not everyone responded that way. Some felt guilty about what they were made to do. One of the other survivors of Auschwitz I know had the job of carrying the bodies back from the crematoria. He would not have done that had some-one not put a gun to his head and forced him. He has been back to the camp three or four times. It's the only vacation he takes. He must keep going back. He has never gotten rid of the guilt. . . . Look, there was even cannibalism in Auschwitz. Some people ate the meat off the buttocks of the dead. I could never go so far, no matter what. I would rather have died.

We were liberated on the twenty-seventh of January, 1945. My brother and I went to Kraków. We met a man there who said he had seen my father, and he was still alive. But then another man came back to Kraków who had been on a train with my father later, and he had been there when my father tried to run away and was shot. So we knew we would never see my father again. I thought if Mother were still alive, she might go back to Radom, so my brother and I went back home. The gentiles who had been living in my house gave it back for us to live in. Our big beautiful piano was still there, but my mother wasn't. Then one morn-ing, three months later, it was the strangest thing. I walked by this open window, and down below in the street I saw my mother walking. I must have screamed because I saw her turn around. I ran down to the street where she was waiting. She looked so small to me and frail. I couldn't believe she was actually back home with me. We stood in the street hugging.

Not much changed in Radom after the war. Only now it was the Russians instead of the Germans. In order to continue to have enough food to put on the table, we had to sell our property. And as soon as there was an edict requiring the Jews to leave, some people told us about it and warned us to get out while we still could. We were well known in Radom. That very night we packed up and left. We had no choice. Besides, we had no roots in Poland anymore. Everyone was gone.

We went to Augsburg, Germany, and stayed with some cousins who had moved there also from Radom. I joined a kibbutz, and I lived there. At the time, I had no preference for what type of Jew I was. I thought about this for the first time. Am I Orthodox? Am I not Orthodox? Am I Conser-vative? Reform? What? I decided it didn't matter, I was Jewish. But as it happened, the organization we joined was very Orthodox. It was all right, because we were united with children our own age. And everyone was Jewish. This was what mattered.

After three of four months, we went on to Stuttgart, where an entire area had been set up for people returning from concentration camps. My mother was given a job in the kitchen where all the children ate lunch and supper. We were given a certain amount of money for our daily living, and our rent was taken care of. A couple of cousins joined us there, so we lived together as one big happy family. One of my cousins even got married there. Under the circumstances, life was as normal as it could be. I went to school from eight o'clock in the morning to six, seven o'clock in the evening. Everybody spoke Yiddish, but we also had a teacher who taught us German. And Polish was being spoken by many of the people, so the languages ended up a conglomeration of everything. Going to school for so many hours was a joy, was heaven. It was wonderful to have something to do other than just wait to be killed the next day. I used to have dates by the hour. Since I couldn't date during the week, when Saturday came, I'd go out with one boy for two hours, then another for two hours, then another. It used to make my mother scream. Germany had beautiful woods, castles, museums. Even going to the library, walking and talking was wonderful. You know, so much had happened to us, and people came from such different backgrounds, it was interesting getting to know them all. Of course, it was a completely different way of dating from the way it is here in the United States. We didn't think about sex, about going to smooch in a car. We were just hungry for fun.

I joined an organization that did not really care what you believed. You were free to do what you wanted; you were Jewish, and that was what mattered. I loved that attitude. Being Orthodox was not my cup of tea. In Poland everybody had been Orthodox. If you didn't go to shul, everybody knew it. We ate kosher meat, lit the candles on Friday nights, my father stayed home on Shabbas. There was no choice. But by this time in my life, though I was grateful for surviving and believed in God very strongly, I wanted to be free, to be able to make my own rules. I belonged to that organization for four years.

In 1949, before we came here, I was taken to the hospital because my right hand was hurting. They said the bone in my thumb was deteriorating from malnutrition. Before they operated, they thought they were going to cut off my whole right hand. When they opened my thumb, they cleaned out the bone, but my hand was spared. Then when we were getting ready to apply for our visas to come to the United States, they said I had lung damage. My mother had to go out and buy ham three times a day for me to eat to cover up the damage. It was life or death. I didn't care whether we moved to Israel or the United States, but if I didn't pass the physical, only my mother and brother would have been able to leave Germany. This country didn't take into consideration that I was a survivor of the concentration camps; they didn't want the responsibility of sick human beings. But by the time we left, I was okay.

After we landed in America, we went to stay with some cousins in New York for a short while, but my mother thought we had no future there. She was very eager to stand on her own two feet, not to be dependent on our cousins who were our sponsors. And that's why we came to Minneapolis. The Jewish Federation there said we could move into a big apartment with another family. We lived with Mrs. Steinberg on Westgarten for three or four months. During that time I was hired for five different jobs, and I got fired from five different jobs, day by day. I had no language, and I had never learned a trade. But finally I found a job at a manufacturer's taking the pieces from the cutters and putting them together so the operators could make them into dresses. My mother also found a job, and my brother went to school.

Mrs. Steinberg's husband introduced me to Manny. He brought him home for supper three days after we arrived. I was nineteen years old, and Manny was twenty-eight. He was from Stuttgart also, but we hadn't known each other before. I met other boys as well, boys from Germany who were also newcomers. Three different men asked me out for New Year's Eve that year, but I had no dress that was right, and I wanted a new dress so badly. I would have had to spend my whole week's allowance that was left after buying food in order to get one. But downstairs from where I was working was a fabric store where I bought a pattern for a dress. I didn't have a sewing machine, and I had no idea how to sew, but I thought if I bought thick fabric and drew a line around the pattern, I would be all right. That dress took me months to make. I had to do it and I did, but I ended up buying a dress for myself anyway. When New Year's Eve came, I still hadn't decided which boy I would go out with, since I had said yes to all three. As it happened, Manny was the first one.

If your own existence is important enough to you, you're going to go out and get what you want. Nothing is going to come to you. I found a job, I found friends. There were good friends, there were bad friends, but they were important to me. But one day when we went to the Jewish Federation, a woman was there, a widow, Mrs. Epstein, very well-to-do. She said she had such a big house and was living there all alone since she had no children of her own, and she invited us to come stay with her. She was just like heaven. She reminded us of the grandmother we never had.

I would go out with another couple boys, but it was always Manny. He was much more mature than the others. When I had enough of having fun, being mature was more important to me in a man. Manny and I went out for a year and four months before we settled down. It was high time; I was nineteen. When we got married, Mrs. Epstein put together the wedding for us and saw to it that her rabbi from her synagogue was there and that we joined the congregation after. It was so great to be part of people, just like being reunited with a family after losing one. It was the beginning of life.

We lived in a free world, but that didn't mean that it couldn't happen to you, that you couldn't still have your freedom taken away. It had just happened, six, seven years before, that I had seen children being killed, and in the back of my mind I still wondered, should I have children? Why would I want to bring children into the world just to be killed? To have pain again? But Manny wanted a child. My doctor said, when he examined me, that I would never have one. But I did not tell my husband that. One month I missed my period, then a second one. Still, my doctor didn't think I could have been pregnant because of the way I was built. I started to bleed very badly one day, and I called him up. He came to our apartment and said I had to go to the hospital because I had just had a miscarriage, and that I had lost the one chance I might have had to give birth to my own child. I suddenly wanted a child more than ever. I wanted to prove that doctor wrong. I went to a new doctor who assured me there was no reason I could not conceive. Within a year I became pregnant again. I worked until I delivered, and I had a normal birth. Everything was fine. That first doctor was wrong, and I have two sons three years apart to prove it.

Manny had his own business making and selling furniture. We could have used my salary, but I thought it was much more important to stay home with the children, so I stayed home. I started going to school during that time. I took the bus and went to a junior college, not for a degree, just to take courses. Then in 1960, my mother died. It hurt me terribly, because she never got any of the things we fought to live for all those years. She was in pain for weeks. Why? Was that necessary? Who do you ask? Who answers those questions?

My mother's death made be bitter, and I became bored with life. I had to get a job. My husband took me to a store to apply for one, but he said they would never hire me. At the time, there were two jobs available, one in the china department, the other in foundations.

I got the job selling foundations. At the time, the salesgirls worked on commission. I had to figure out a way to sell more than the others. Then I got this idea. I went into the costume room, which I loved; I loved beautiful dresses. I put on a dress that was a size ten, even though I really wore a size fourteen. Then I went up to the women shopping in the costume room, told them what I had done and that if they'd put on a longline bra and two girdles, one medium and one small, they could fit into a size ten too! My sales jumped up, and within six months I was the highest selling salesperson there. I worked four days a week, four hours a day. One day a vice-president of the company came up to me and said, "You are not going to stay just a saleslady. You have made a revolution in this store. The way you talk with your customers, the way you think, you should apply for a manager's position at one of the other branch stores of our company. I know where there's an opening." But when I went for an interview and found out how much responsibility I'd have, and how little money I'd be making, I turned it down. The vice-president called me the next day, and when I explained, he said he would make an opening for me as a manager at the same store where I was already working, his store, and he'd pay me more money.

Eventually I became an assistant buyer, then a buyer. But that didn't last too long, because my husband objected terribly to this. He had heard that if you're a buyer and go to New York, you have to sleep with the president of the company, sell yourself for your job. And then he said, "How can you leave your children and destroy your home life for your career?" Well, I cried for twenty-four hours, but I knew that my position as a mother and wife was more important than my buyer's position. So I went back to the store as a manager. I was mad at my husband, but you cannot live with a man with all that bitterness. It took me a few months to get over that. I believed that with no degree, no training, no influence, just on determination alone, I could have reached the pinnacle of my opportunities. But from his point of view, I had brought children into this world, and I had other responsibilities.

I went to a social worker at this time. She asked me if I ever considered divorce. I said, "Not once. He is the father of my children, he puts bread and butter on the table. He is a good man." He just couldn't bring himself to tell me he was worried about my sleeping with another man, and I know that jealousy had a lot to do with it, aside from his worry about the children. If I am born again, I am going to be born as a man. Regardless of how far women go in the women's movement, if you are married, the man can still insist that your responsibility is to your children. If a woman has a job and a man has a job, the man still has the upper hand.

I have always been a fighter. Just like in the camps. You do what you have to do. When I was manager, I used to say, "Why can't the next person work as hard as I do?" I used to be angry about it. I used to be frustrated not knowing how to motivate or stimulate another individual. That's what my bleeding ulcer came from. I am not a perfectionist, but when I have a job to do, I will do it to the best of my ability. People should think about what they are doing day in and day out, but I had to learn the hard way that not everybody does this. They think just being on the job is enough. But what have they accomplished? When I have a job, raising children or cooking a meal, I want to give all of me or nothing. But those are things that I'm not going to take home anymore. I'm not going to have another bleeding ulcer.

Nowadays when I'm standing there selling foundations, such a boring job, I know how far I could have gone. I'm still sorry, but I had the satisfaction of knowing what I was able to do. My ability was recognized, and that's a step in the right direction.

Still, the job serves me in two ways. There are some mornings that I cannot get up from bed because for the past three years I have had MS. But I am able to say to myself, "You have to go to your job." And just thinking that makes me get up, makes me be strong. And second of all, we have a fantastic hospitalization program for employees. And being as sick as I am, knowing that I have a doctor on call at all times means an awful lot.

But I tell you, now with this disease I have, I'm not sure I want to go on fighting. I'm not sure if it's going to be worth it. I can't stand not to be able to control myself. It's getting harder for me to talk, my eyes tear constantly. I don't have good control of my bladder. And the worst thing is my walk. I have to hold onto somebody or something. Sometimes, especially if the ground's uneven, I fall. But I still drive myself; I go where I need to go. I can't stand being dependent. I will never be an invalid. Today I went to buy a friend a present. Could you imagine if I couldn't do those things, if I had to say, "Take me here, take me there?" I might as well be six feet underground. I would only become a burden to other people. I refuse to think about using a wheelchair. I think if that happens I will commit suicide. I mean it. I will not go on living if I can't walk on my own two feet. No, life would not be worth fighting for then. In Auschwitz when people couldn't walk, the next step was dying. And such a horrible way to die. They took the blood out of children too weak to get out of bed. Then the next day they took them out to the trucks that picked up the bodies.

I am not afraid of pain; my body can withstand pain. Recently I had problems with my root canals. When I went to the dentist, he said it was so bad he didn't see how I could have stood it for so long, the pain. I had let it go so long he had to pull all my teeth out. I am not afraid of dying either. Seeing another dead body meant nothing to us. People were dying by the truckloads, simply thrown into the fire. What did one more mean? At Birkenau there were too many bodies to know what to do with them all. That's why they made the crematoria. Nobody wanted us. Not even the United States. We were nobody. We were totally helpless, like ants walking on the ground. All my mother could do was pick lice off her children. She tried to give us some of her rations, but we wouldn't take them. I know what it's like to have no satisfaction in life, just the power of thinking I would be able to survive. I will not live that way again.

Sometimes after work in the afternoons, I have to lie down and rest. But I hate it. My days are not long enough. There is so much I want to accomplish. I would love to go back to painting. A friend of mine came over for lunch, and I showed her some of my paintings. She said, "You've got it. Go back to this." But I tell you, when I come home from working, I'm so drained that I cannot do it anymore. Besides, the art that I do is very morbid art. It is not the kind of art that anyone would buy to hang on their walls. But I have to continue working. My doctor says it's the only thing that keeps me going, the responsibility to get out of bed. I hold onto the furniture to make it into the kitchen. Many times I will say, "Why me?" But then I get up and say, "But that's the way it is." What can I do? There's nothing to do.

One more life doesn't make a difference. I only fear having to go to a wheelchair. Other than that, I am not afraid of anything. Sometimes if we're out for supper at someone's home, if I've been sitting too long, I get up and stretch out on the floor. Eventually the pain goes away. But I don't like to complain. What's the point of screaming or carrying on? No one would listen to me or help. I'd just wear myself out. I am the only one who has to be responsible for my own existence. That is the way it has always been. I live with bitterness, but not with anger. What is there to feel sad about? That I have gone through the Holocaust? It was just part of my life. It was not me. It was everybody. Everybody that was born a Jew. I was one amongst them. I am not mourning.

My brother was lucky to escape with his life. All they did was experiment on him with shots so that he could recover. Not recover, exactly. He has never recovered. He lived to come to this country when he was fourteen. He went to school and college. He's a very bright individual who can learn fast and adapt to situations. But after he graduated from college, he couldn't keep a job. Something always drove him away. Since my mother passed away in 1960, he's been to four or five different cities. With the money he makes, he goes to Spain, to Portugal, to Germany. In 1962 they found him lying on the streets in Israel. The mental institution took him in, and he's there now. They found him an apartment, and he's on a working schedule. But he can't have the responsibility of staying with a job. He can't sleep at night, because all he's been through comes back to him. He goes back to the hospital for observation, then back out again. Whatever the Nazi doctors did to him and put into his body made him the way he is today.

I came to the United States, and I am a happy individual. I have a husband and children. If I get aggravated with them, we can talk about it and do something about it. I appreciate little things like this more than people. I didn't have the freedom of speech, the freedom of expression before I moved to this country. Not to have "Big Brother" looking over me is so great that this is what makes me happy. And I'm going to be as happy as I can be while I'm on this earth.

5
Naomi

Naomi is one of the lucky ones. She and her parents escaped from Germany without experiencing either camp or ghetto. Naomi agreed to be interviewed for this book out of respect for my interest in her story, although she believed her story was not within the scope of this book. She insisted that the word survivor *did not apply to her; she did not suffer enough. She speaks and looks thoroughly American and has a cheerful, self-assured, energetic, and appealing manner. I believed that Naomi had a great deal to contribute to this project, and I hoped that she would benefit from it as well. Before our interviews began, I was aware that the Holocaust was an overwhelming and constant presence in Naomi's thoughts, a fixation she attributed to her genetic predisposition for morbidity. She attended community and cultural events centered around the Holocaust, read books and articles on the topic, spoke and wrote about her ever-present turmoil in trying to come to terms with the subject. Yet she denied that her concern was different from anyone else's, that her early years had anything to do with her obsession. Since our interviews, Naomi is less obsessed with the Holocaust. She has become president of a Jewish community organization that focuses on human rights. Naomi speaks for all the children who escaped the physical tortures of the ghettos and camps, but grew up in an atmosphere that bred insecurity and confusion during the psychologically crucial developmental years.*

I have to tell you I'm not sure that the existential despair I have lived with all these years was necessarily a derivative of all my early experiences. There have always been people like me. It was a terrible gloom I was born into, but there have been other grim times. There are some pretty grim happenings around us now. It just takes a special talent to concentrate on the grimness. I really think it's a biological predisposition to think this way, supported and reinforced by all the wrong people. In terms of the Holocaust, I didn't really have any personal trauma. I remember so little about those times. I wish I could remember more. There are so many empty spaces. I was seven years old when we left Germany, and I've repressed so much. But there isn't a day when the Holocaust doesn't haunt me. I've tried to write about it, but I just can't say what I really want to say. Yet I can't seem to let go of it either. I feel compelled to watch every movie made about it, to read about it constantly, to be aware always that it happened.

I came out of the Holocaust totally unscathed, physically. I never saw a concentration camp. I can't defend my depression on the basis of my experiences. It's not what happened to me—I don't even remember what happened to me—that fills my head. It's purely existential, knowing what humanity is capable of in terms of inflicting pain and suffering on others. I can't come to terms with that. There is no joy, no pleasure that comes my way that can overcome for a fleeting instant the awareness of that awful truth.

My mother, being the kind of person she is, says nothing bad has ever happened to her. To this day she won't think about my grandmother having been taken to a concentration camp, having stood at the edge of a grave she probably had to dig herself; she just won't think about that. My mother doesn't get depressed; she has a guardian angel who watches over her. I'm the one who thinks about all of this and worries. How much of this had to do with the war, and how much was a personal style that would have happened anyway, I can't know. But I will talk with you about my experiences in Germany and after since you think I have something to say.

My parents' backgrounds were very ordinary. Mother went to grade school and then to a Jewish school for girls, a trade school. My father went to a gymnasium. They were raised to emulate the high German Jewish culture. My maternal grandmother always said if you couldn't afford to go to the play, at least you could read the reviews. Both my mother and my father came from families with a lot of cultural and educational aspirations, not matched by their achievements. My aunt, my mother's only living relative, tells the story of my grandparents receiving the news that my mother was pregnant, not many months after my parents were married.

According to my aunt, my grandmother was horrified that I was going to be born during such troubled times. I don't think my parents had planned the pregnancy. I was born in 1930, nine months and ten days after my parents were married. My mother was only nineteen years old. She and my father lived in Hagen, a little town in Germany, but my mother went home to Hamburg to be with her mother when it was time for me to be born. I was an only child until I was fourteen years old, when we were living in the United States. My mother became pregnant in between, when I was six or seven, but she had an illegal abortion. She went on the train alone and came home alone, and almost bled to death, though I knew nothing of this at the time.

There wasn't a lot of physical warmth or caring given to me. I was never cuddled. My mother never had the instincts for mothering, and she was so young. Mother doesn't give praise easily, and if she does there's a barb in it. I remember her saying, "Mrs. So and So thinks you're pretty, but I don't know . . ." Years later, when I asked why she had said something that had hurt me so much, she said she didn't want me to be conceited. She certainly succeeded in achieving that goal for me. Everything I did she questioned. "Why don't you do it this way?" she'd say. My decisions or methods were never really supported. When I was still very young, some people came to visit with a baby, and I gave the baby a plum. They must have said, "How could you have given the baby a plum?" I know I felt that I had really done something wrong, because much later, after they'd left our house and gone back home, weeks, maybe months later I heard that the baby had died, and I thought I had killed the baby by giving it that plum. I've always believed war, peace, it was my fault.

When I was two, we moved from Hagen to Büende. I don't think there were very many Jewish families in town, maybe a dozen. My father had a textile business which was connected to our living quarters, which had been a cigar factory, and the bars of the factory had been left on the windows. I remember when my parents left me alone at night, I felt afraid and fantasized that the door might get stuck, and if I needed to get out I wouldn't be able to, not even out of the windows because of the bars, and I'd imagine that someone could slip candy to me under the door so I wouldn't starve. Nonpareils we used to call those candies in German, "pearls of love."

As we're talking, I can see the courtyard of our building, and a garden with chickens and gooseberries and currants, and in the corner an iron gate I went through to get to school. I can see myself standing there with a young girl who lived near me, the daughter of a storm trooper. She always stood with her skirt hiked up on one side, her left hand holding onto her underpants, the way other kids might clutch a blanket or a teddy bear. Her name was Waltraut Ruschenpoehler. Funny that I can remember her name. I was taught to be cautious around her, not to tell her too much about us, although her father knew we were Jewish anyway. She was the only friend I can remember in Büende.

My mother told me that when I was three years old, which seems ridiculously young for her to have sent me to do something like this, she told me to go to the store across the street to buy something for her, and I didn't come back for the longest time, much longer than it should have taken, in her estimation. Later I explained that I had gone to a second store because the first one didn't have the item she wanted. She gave me a lot of praise for having shown such initiative and repeated the story proudly to me when I got older, although I don't remember the incident myself or any feeling of power or gratification. I don't remember ever having felt that while I was growing up.

My father was mainly interested in business, and I saw him as the breadwinner, someone I didn't notice much until I was an adolescent. He spent his time doing a few things well and wasn't interested as my mother was in expanding his range of knowledge. I do remember that my father and mother used to go for motorcycle rides until they had an accident once. He never took me with him on his motorcycle, which was just as well. I probably would have been too afraid. One incident between my father and myself stands out vividly in my memory. It was before Chanukah, and my father shared with me what he was going to get my mother for a present. I felt it was a moment of trust between us. But when Chanukah came, the present he gave my mother turned out to be something entirely different from the secret he had shared with me, and I realized that he hadn't, in fact, trusted me with the truth. It was a terrible blow to me because I remember how upset I was about that. I'm sure I never told him how upset I was, but I decided then not to believe what my parents told me.

I was a serious kid from the word go. From my earliest years, I could see ethical ramifications to situations and felt I had to be absolutely moral and righteous. I think I realized what a disappointment I was to my mother, not being the kind of child she would have wanted, with a child's sense of joy and fun. Even as a child, I never got excited about having things, possessions. When I was five or six years old, my mother bought me a fantastic doll buggy for Chanukah. Now she loved dolls; in fact, when she left home to get married, she took one of her favorite dolls with her. I never really cared about dolls myself. But my mother was very exicted about the buggy she had bought me for Chanukah and hid it in the back of the store where we lived. She told me later that she had counted the days 'til she could give it to me so she could see my face when I saw it. Chanukah came, and she took me to the place where she had hidden the buggy, expecting to see me light up with joy and enthusiasm, but all I said was "Why is there paper on those wheels of the doll's carriage?" I really didn't care about the doll buggy.

I don't remember doing things with my mother, except on Sunday afternoons my parents used to take me to a coffeehouse in a nearby town. I was a pretty child and small for my age, and the people who met at the coffeehouse to drink and talk used to pass me around from lap to lap petting me, making over me. I felt pretty, flirting with the men there. My mother used to tease me that I was needful of that kind of attention, which she found funny. It was nice, being important and the center of so much attention. It didn't happen very often.

During several summers, I went to stay with my grandmother in Hamburg. She used to take me places, to the store at her street corner, for instance. I remember her cutting off wedges of the cucumbers to see if they were bitter, and I still remember the smell of roasting coffee on the streets of Hamburg. I can visualize the precise arrangement of her apartment and some of the children who were neighbors. I remember being happy with my grandmother. One day at her house, I choked on some chicken skin, but it was my grandmother who picked me up and slapped me on the back. She was the one who saved me.

My great-grandfather lived in the same building with my grandparents in Hamburg. He was around a lot. We had seders with him at his apartment. He loved pepper and spicy foods, which became my excuse for loving them too, since he lived to a ripe old age. I suspect he was the most loving person in my life. When he died, of course, I wasn't allowed to attend the funeral. I doubt my parents even told me he was dead. He just disappeared. That's what happened all those years after; people just disappeared. No one explained to me; no one told me anything.

Jewishly, I think my family was really sympathetic to the German Reform movement. Nobody was that religious, though we never denied our Judaism. My mother to this day doesn't wash clothes on Shabbas, and we never ate forbidden foods, though we didn't keep kosher. We lit candles on Friday night and observed the holidays, but there was no hint of Orthodoxy. My grandparents were the same way; there was no break in tradition between my parents' generation and their parents! We had a synagogue in our town which probably drew from all the little towns around it and to which we belonged. One Chanukah I was chosen to read a poem to our congregation. I can see myself standing on a soapbox which was about as big as I was, reciting. The poem was called "Der Diener," which means servant. Recently I came across a copy of the poem and translated it into English. It's a morbid little poem now that I look back on it, especially for a five-year-old to be asked to recite.

The Servant

With its flame the burning candle
Sets the other eight aglow
And for that it earns the title
Just of servant, nothing more.
Set off harshly from the others,
Kept from mingling with its brothers,
In a world made somewhat brighter
Because it gladly shares its light—
This little candle stands alone.

And so it is with my sad people
As it goes with that small light
In whose shimmering, wavering flames
The whole of Jewish history glows.
Having lit the human spirit
With the purest flame of God,
Our poor people's doomed forever
To serve and serve and serve.

There was a lot of anti-Semitism in my grade school, teachers who were known to be Nazis. The teacher we got when we started school moved through the grades with us, and the teacher in the class behind me was a real Jew hater. This provided a strong incentive for me to do well in school, because if I flunked, I would have gone to this Nazi teacher's class, and I certainly didn't want to end up with her. There were no other Jewish children in my class. I remember coming home very excited one day because we had gotten special cookies in school since it was Hitler's birthday. After 1938, I wasn't permitted back in school.

My parents never discussed with me the difficulties in the world. And of course they knew only what was in the papers, which was so little of the truth. The climate was such that they wouldn't have told me much, even if they had known. "The walls have ears" was the saying in Germany at the time. Children were known to betray their parents' plans, accidentally or intentionally. Perhaps this contributed to my parents' lack of communication with me. Eventually the laws required my father to sell his business to a gentile businessman. One day while my mother and I were visiting my grandparents in Hamburg, and my father was at home in

Büende, some neighbors came to my grandparents' apartment and began telling stories about husbands and fathers who had disappeared, had been taken away by storm troopers. I don't remember this, but my mother says I had an anxiety attack and had to go to bed. I must have been scared to death from all those stories I was hearing, frightened that my father too would disappear and that I'd be left alone. I'd always worried about being abandoned.

My mother and her sister-in-law went to the train station in Hamburg to look for my father. Unbelievably, my mother saw him hanging onto the outside of a streetcar. He told us later that while he was in Büende, the storm troopers, who were not from our town and therefore didn't know anyone, came to our house with lists of people they were looking for and asked my father if his name was Katz. My father simply told them that was not his name, and they left. He got out of the house and immediately went to the train station, realizing this was his last chance to get away. This was Kristallnacht.

When my father arrived with my mother and my aunt, my grandmother insisted that we all stay in the back of her apartment. But it was the men who were in danger of being rounded up and taken at that point. My father wasn't supposed to go to the door or stand near the window, but after a couple of days of feeling so trapped, he said he was going to turn himself in if it meant continuing to live like that. At the time my grandfather was working for a department store. The SS had come to take away some of his superiors in his presence, so he was scared to death and had his suitcase ready in case the knock came to his door and he had to go with them. But the knock just didn't come then. I don't know why, because it came to neighbors on their street. We were just lucky.

After Kristallnacht, as a natural follow-up to all the havoc, the SS went to our apartment in Büende. The gentile man who had bought my father's business told the police that all the property was his, so they wouldn't destroy any of our possessions. Nonetheless, the SS came in and rummaged through our things, taking with them some letters from my mother's desk, among which was a love letter, a poem written to her by an admiring man she knew. Mother had always had some male friend hanging around. My father found her so lovable he enjoyed the admiration from others with her, and he knew the relationships were platonic. When the Nazis found the letters written to my mother, they hung them up in an exhibit to demonstrate the low culture of the Jews.

My mother knew the letters were gone. I, of course, didn't know anything about what the Nazis had taken, or about the exhibit later. But recently my mother recited the poem that had been displayed with such contempt in the anti-Semitic exhibit, and I wrote it down and translated it.

Though I'm clearly far from being
Goethe, Schiller or Heine,
I can still set my thoughts to verse
As well as I'm inclinedta.
Still, no monument will come my way,
No prizes gold or regal
I might as well write this poem today
Just for Rosa Seigel.

To you I dedicate these lines
And thank you from the heart
For the lovely hours we shared
In laughter and repartee.

You've made me young again—
Younger than I've ever been.
I feast on the memory of you and ask,
Without scintilla of sin,
Will your husband travel more?
The housefriend stays in place,
And won't be easily dismissed
Will you go along?
It's what I call a marriage à trois.

I don't know if my mother felt violated or if she felt proud of being made famous by the Nazis. I certainly felt violated when I heard about it. At the time of Kristallnacht and after, I must have observed the fact that my parents were both upset, although I didn't expect to be told what was happening or let in on adult conversations. I certainly must have been pretty scared, but I didn't ever tell my parents things like that when they were worried about protecting our lives.

My father went back to see the damage created by the SS in our apartment, and then eventually we all went back, packed up our belongings, and left Büende and Germany. Years before, my father had made inquiry of the United States consul asking how to get to this country, and they had sent him information. He was incredibly slow at making decisions, so by the time we applied it was late and there weren't ten Jews in Germany not on a waiting list to emigrate. But my father's application number had been issued before, from his first request for information, which is what saved us as it put us high on the list.

It was amazing that the Germans were still letting the Jews leave. The single restriction was that we could only take ten U.S. dollars with us out of the country. Before we left, my parents were able to buy furniture, clothes for me, and three tickets to New York and Chicago. I vaguely remember that we got the word that our papers had been finalized and had to go to Stuttgart on the way to Holland to catch the boat for the United States. Evidently we had some wealthy relative in Chicago who had signed an affidavit for us. A couple of my father's brothers had preceded us already, and this is how we settled in Chicago. I think I left Germany relatively carefree. I don't think I understood the significance of leaving, the distances. My grandparents stayed in Germany, but I expected them to come to America later. I enjoyed the trip across the ocean. There were other children on the boat, and I remember having a costume event planned for us. My mother got sick during the crossing, and my father stayed below with her, so I ate in the dining room by myself. I don't think I minded it, socializing with strangers, feeling very grown-up and independent, ordering tea with lemons. I remember New York was such a mob scene, and I missed seeing the Statue of Liberty because we were with some customs officials on the other side of the boat with predisembarkment business to attend to.

From New York we took a bus to Chicago to join my father's brother and his family, although once we got to this country, our wealthy relatives didn't have much to do with us. They felt they had done everything necessary already. I remember the first day on Humboldt Avenue in Chicago, going downstairs to play with some American kids. The first English word I learned, I learned from them, "Shutup!" What could I have said to make them say that to me? Cheese? Table? Hello, maybe.

We lived in Chicago from 1939 to 1943. My parents both worked, and I was more isolated than ever. I remember having fever, being delirious and being left alone even then. I had to learn a new language and was forever getting lost on the way home from school, being teased by other children. I really raised myself and was always aware that my parents had their own tremendous burdens to carry. Another one of my father's brothers had been in a concentration camp and had been shot trying to escape. While we were living in Chicago, the Red Cross contacted us to say that my uncle was starving in China, would we save him? He came to stay with us for a while, though we were living in pretty minimal accommodations ourselves. Even though my parents knew more of the language than I did when we moved here, quickly I assumed the role of shielding them. They didn't come to my school for activities, I never brought friends home, and I never really told them my business. Emotionally, I cut them off from my life.

The last letter from my grandmother came in 1941, probably just before she and my grandfather were deported and murdered. I still have the letter which she wrote on the back of printed instructions regarding emigration to the United States. The letter looks very strange, with the print cut around so that no extra unused paper shows. I don't know if she did this to emphasize something, to indicate more than would have gotten past the censors, or whether she cut the paper this way for the sake of economy.

My sweet Naomi!

I believe that you have totally forgotten your Oma and Opa. I have written you so often, but you have never answered. What do you do all day? How many girlfriends do you actually have? And which classroom do you honor with your little persona? I mean, the way we are used to knowing you. How are Ruth and Alfred? And do you get together with them often?

My sweet Naomi, it is very nice for you to read good books, but you must also play with your schoolmates. One is soon enough grown up, and then playtime is done with, and then one would often gladly play and longs to return to one's childhood again. Do you know Opa says every morning: soon I'll be able to go to Chicago with my Naomi; she'll show us everything beautiful, and I will eat chocolate and ice-cream with Naomi forever. That will be a glorious life. Best of all, he would like to buy all of Hamburg for you. But he always says, do you think that Naomi still prays for us the way she always used to do here? The dear God always fulfills children's prayers! So my beloved Naomi, stay always a good girl, Kisses from the heart from

your Oma and Opa

What really hurt was when she said, "You never write." We wrote all the time but they never got the mail. They couldn't really tell us what was happening, so we have no way of knowing what anguish they suffered, but we know it was November of 1941 when the Nazis came and took my grandparents away. It's an overwhelming sadness when I think of my grandmother, but I just can't remember her as she was, I can't visualize her face, though surely I wasn't too young to remember.

As news dribbled in, letters came, I became aware of what was happening in Europe. It became clear to me that if we hadn't been fortunate enough to come here something awful could have happened to me. What would have happened? How would I have reacted? Could I have withstood suffering? Or what if I had to face this in the future? I used to test myself physically in minor ways, without actually doing myself harm; overheating the bathwater, holding my finger into the flame of a candle just to see how much stress, physical or mental, I could endure, whatever situation presented itself, pushing to the limits.

From the time we moved to this country, there wasn't a secure word out of my father's mouth. He always said he was on the verge of losing his job, which really frightened me, though I don't think this threat was a reality. We call it the Spiegel streak, this lack of confidence in himself. I always thought he was smarter than he thought he was, and I used to blame my mother for his insecurities because she dominated him, rushed in to fill the gaps, finished his sentences. In contrast to her energy and dynamism, he became more and more placid. He asked her how to brush his teeth when he got up in the mornings.

When I started school in Chicago, I was eight years old, but the administration wanted me to start over in kindergarten, which was a real affront to my dignity. We compromised on first grade, which was reasonable since I didn't know English. There were no other immigrants in my school, no special efforts made in my behalf, either I kept up or I didn't. I began to accelerate quickly, and every six months or so I'd change grades. We also moved several times during those years we lived in Chicago, so I never established any real friendships or lasting ties. That was what I missed most in my childhood. And I never felt like I belonged. I was eight or nine years old, one child of many who had been surrounded by the threat of physical danger, put into a new environment and told suddenly, ''Okay, now you shouldn't think about anything more than hamburgers and ABCs.'' But I never would have even thought to complain. After all, look how lucky I was compared to the children in Europe. I had my life, what was there to complain about?

In 1944, we moved to St. Louis because of a job change for my father. I think it was in the alley between Rosebury and Southwood in St. Louis that the dawn of recognition came to me that my life didn't really matter, in the greater scheme of things.

When I first heard that my mother was pregnant, I didn't believe it. I was in junior high school at the time, and maybe I was embarrassed by the news, but frankly I don't think I knew about sex. What I do remember is that I didn't expect the pregnancy to lead to a baby. It came as a real shock when this new person arrived. I had prepared myself for disaster all my years. Maybe my mother would die from this pregnancy. But when my sister was born and I went down to the hospital, she was the most beautiful baby there and everything was wonderful. I just don't remember having any negative feelings about her, although my aunt has always suggested that I must have felt tremendous sibling rivalry with my new sister, but I can tell you that I never felt she took anything away from me. I didn't have anything anyway in terms of attention. If there was a change for me, it was that she took some pressure off me. I babysat with her and I enjoyed it. She was a relative I could be close to, and I feel this way about her to this very day.

Going through high school, I continued to feel alienated from my peers, although I was very involved in activities and to the outside world probably seemed like a very normal teenager. I coped well, except that I had trouble sleeping and sometimes would have heart palpitations that I thought were heart attacks and were going to kill me before I was twenty. Looking back, I know that I never really dealt with my past experiences, my background, emotionally. I just coped.

I also fought a lot with my father during this time. Not about specific issues that I can remember. He was a very placid man who never got angry, except at home when he would suddenly explode on occasion. I think my temperament is much like his and he would shout at me that he was right about something and I would think that I was right, although in fights between him and my mother I generally side with him.

I never felt really miserable or sad or angry. I was never aware of any feelings I had or any real expectations from life. I never complained, just reacted with this flat emotional response. That may have been what I was doing all along since I was a child, protecting myself from my emotions. Of course I never really missed feelings, I just kept trudging along being the best little girl I could be. I do not blame my parents for any of this. They did the best they could raising me, but they had so much to deal with themselves.

When I decided to get married, it was a very rational decision since I didn't know what else to do and was nineteen years old, the same age my mother was when she married my father. I didn't want to be a burden to my parents any more and I thought the man I was going to marry would be good balance for me; he would provide stability, warmth, people skills, all the things I didn't have. And now I'm awfully glad I did. When you think about how many marriages in the past were arranged for good genetic stock, that didn't end in divorce as so many marriages now do, I arranged mine in the same way, as a sound intellectual decision.

I had a four-year scholarship to college, but my husband said, ''Let's get married and you'll go to work,'' which is what I did. I didn't know where I was going in the world anyway. There wasn't anything I wanted to have or to do or to be. It goes back to that insight I had had in the alley when I was fourteen, ''It doesn't matter. I'm alive. What more could I want?''

A teacher wrote in my high school yearbook, ''We expect you to be the first woman senator from Missouri.'' I still live with the fact that I didn't meet that expectation. Whatever anybody wanted me to do, I did. I had no way of defining my own wants or needs and sometimes that put a lot of pressure on me because different people wanted me to do different things. That's why having children was hard, I couldn't please them all at the same time and I didn't know what I wanted myself.

I never thought I wanted children, I said I didn't need them to make my life complete. It was part of my excessive objectivity. I didn't know how to get excited about people or myself. I envied other people who said they had the best mother in the world, or the best car, the best anything. I never felt that, only this continuing negative self-image, and I didn't want to pass on all my troubles to the next generation.

When I had children and all the pressures of mothering, I began to feel myself falling apart. I didn't think I was good enough, couldn't be a perfect mother, didn't know how to ask for help. I had absolutely no support whatsoever. My husband worked seven days a week for some periods during the year and sometimes didn't come home until 10:30 at night. He was always busiest in January, including traveling. Then I was really alone with all the responsibilities of the children and the house. And I didn't have a car. Even if I had left, I wouldn't have known where to go. There was no place I wanted to be. I never had fantasies. I only thought, I'm here and I'm going to explode. It took me a long time to recognize that at the end of January I'd end up in the hospital thinking I had colitis or appendicitis or something wrong with my gall bladder. I always thought I was dying. Then I'd find out I was fine and go home. Nobody said, "It's going to be okay, you're doing a good job." Nobody ever suggested that I ought to do something about my depression. It just seemed like something hanging around my neck that I lived with, my motor always racing out of control. I don't think I ever knew what serenity was.

When my son went to his first day of first grade. I was thirty-two years old, with three children. I watched Billy go off to school and I was wiped out. I thought I was through, there was nothing I could do in life ever again. I went to bed and felt like I would never get up. Naturally I did get up again when he came home. I always met everybody's expectations.

I didn't exude warmth and I still don't. It's the survivor's burden. You can't take life lightly. The best gift a parent can give a child is sharing laughter, and that was never part of my family's experience. When my daughter called to tell me she was pregnant, and I know she wanted me to be so excited for her, well I wasn't excited, I was scared for her. I couldn't get excited. It was like a leap back in time to the way I felt about having children myself. I wasn't able to give my daughter very much love or support when she was small. It doesn't have to be Nazi Germany for children to be deprived. It's hard to pass on what you haven't gotten yourself. But our grandchild is wonderful and perfect, and my daughter is so happy and doing so well. I said I never needed grandchildren, but this has turned out to be such a lovely surprise! I am so amazed when things turn out well. Though when I hear the anxiety to my daughter's voice sometimes, just the way I used to feel, I can hardly stand it. I feel it twice over again.

Over the years I tried to get help from a variety of professionals. They never wanted to deal with the issues I wanted to deal with, issues I felt were important, like the Holocaust. A lot of people know about the Holocaust but their attitude was, why does it have to bother you? Let's talk about your toilet training. I used to get a burning sensation in my mouth, the smell of burning. When I think about what I could have associated with that, I know that on Kristallnacht our synagogue was set on fire. I didn't see it since I was in Hamburg at the time, but my father was president of our congregation and he must have talked about it. And I also knew they burned bodies in the ovens. That must have scared me, too. No one ever asked me about this before.

The psychiatrist who is now my pill pusher would say that I have a pattern of hitting a peak and then getting over it which is genetically and physiologically determined and there's nothing I can do about it. He prescribed Dalmane and Librium. For a while I was taking 100 milligrams a day of Librium while I was working, just to keep me going. It didn't make me drowsy, just less agitated. I tried a lot of other medications over the years, too. Some I could tolerate, some I couldn't.

I went back to school several times in a variety of fields, attempting to find myself, and for a while I worked, but even then I didn't know who I was, what I was doing, where I was going. I didn't know what I was going to be when I grew up or how to justify living. No career was important enough to make a difference in the world. I never wanted a car, a stereo, a trip, although I have those things. It's difficult for me to allow myself pleasure. The fact that I came out of Nazi Germany with nothing terrible happening to me is such a tremendous obligation to justify my own existence or do something positive with it, by action and accomplishment, by making the world a better place, I feel I owe the world something.

As we've been going over all of this, sometimes it depressed me more to think of the thousands, millions who have gone through horrific experiences and somehow triumphed by surviving with confidence in their rage, while I, who suffered no concrete trauma, couldn't conquer the sense of defeat, the lack of spirit I've always felt. It has been impossible for me to get angry with anyone; not with the policeman in an unmarked car who ran into my aunt last year and killed her, not with the doctor who killed my father while performing routine surgery on him a few years ago.

Naomi

Once you have come to the abyss, it's hard to turn your eyes back to the mountaintop, yet facing my experiences as we discussed them in this way I would have to say has been good for me. In spite of the increased depression it caused, some nights I would wake up with some new insights about my life and feel a sense of rightness about them, and some release from my obsession with the Holocaust. I'm even beginning to see why I fit into this group of women you're writing about, women who were very young children living in Nazi Europe who were too young to understand, or too young to remember. In the past year and a half since we began talking, I'm really doing so much better. I haven't used medication at all during this time. I'm even excited about a new job I've taken. I think I'm really moving ahead. Of course I still believe that it's all irrelevant, what happened to me in the greater picture. What matters is that the Holocaust took place and that human beings made it happen. But the guilt for that does not belong to me, except as a part of humanity. I am only one individual. A few years ago a rabbi said to me, "No one of us is God, no one is that responsible." I don't have to be responsible for all the evil in the world. It's a good lesson and I'm trying to remember it.

6
Frederika

Frederika was born in Bratislav, Slovakia, the child of a Jewish father and a non-Jewish mother. Abandoned by her mother, she was sent from camp to camp, her true identity never known by the Nazis. Naoma Zimmerman, a social worker and friend who knew of my intention to write this book, made me aware of Frederika's story. With Frederika's approval, Mrs. Zimmerman sent me tape-recorded copies of several sessions triggered by Frederika's panic over the threatened neo-Nazi marches in Skokie, Illinois, where she was living at the time. After listening to the tapes, I was eager to meet Frederika and interview her myself. By this time, Frederika had moved to South Carolina with her family and was no longer in treatment. According to Mrs. Zimmerman, Frederika was enthusiastically waiting to meet me and contribute what she could to this project. But that meeting never occurred. When Wayne State University Press accepted the manuscript proposal for this book, I called Mrs. Zimmerman and learned that Frederika had died. Her heart attack was attributed to the progress of scleroderma, a disease from which she had suffered for fifteen years. Scleroderma is a degenerative disease in which the skin hardens and becomes rigid, and other organs such as the heart, liver, and kidneys become involved as well. Distressed by the news, I decided to use the information available to me on the existing tapes and include her story as planned, knowing it was her wish that I do so. Frederika was fifty-one years old when she died.

I was struck by the childlike quality of Frederika's voice as I came to know it on my tape recorder. My impression was that it was a struggle for her to be speaking in English, although she came to the United States at a fairly young age and her intellectual capacity was quite good. Frederika did not want to become too much a part of this culture, too American. She chose not to become an American citizen or perfect her English. She said, "This is not home to me. When I say 'home,' I mean Bratislav, Slovakia."

As an adult, Frederika's discomfort with the English language reflected her lack of trust in her new environment in the United States. She did not want to speak about the Holocaust, as if by not uttering the English words for painful memories, she might leave her past behind, buried in Slovak. In describing her experiences, she did not use words common to other survivors, words such as ghetto, concentration camp, *or* SS officer. *These omissions, or little silences, are important in understanding Frederika. For six years during childhood, she did not speak at all. Her silence began in Terezin as an act of rage directed at her mother and continued throughout her years of imprisonment and beyond. Silence was an act of resistance she sustained with anyone she perceived as the enemy.*

The skeletal appearance created by scleroderma reduced her once again to looking like the cadavers that peopled her youth. Scleroderma causes the tissues around the mouth to pull back so that the teeth become prominent in a perpetual grimace. The eyes assume a fixed stare. Frederika described her mother as being "like a skeleton, with two bones sticking out." Children died daily at Terezin and Auschwitz; the living looked like corpses. After the war, Frederika was sickly looking, "horrible. Tall like I am now and skin and bones." Her father also retained a skeletal appearance to Frederika, "with dead eyes looking out." He indicated that Frederika was a living corpse herself, empty on the inside. Eventually, as her disease progressed, she became that living corpse, entombed within her own body, her skin turned to stone. The etiology of scleroderma is unknown and the course of the disease unpredictable. There is little information concerning it in the psychiatric literature, although a relationship between the disease and emotions is described in clinical case studies. Frederika's early symptoms—the choking and the feeling of something running down her leg—indicate a connection between the symptoms of her disease and her experiences in the concentration camps. Frederika connected a physical sensation with her emotional pain, saying, "I have this pinch over my heart." This statement can be seen as a foreshadowing of the heart attack that caused her death.

After Frederika and her family moved to South Carolina, the relationship between Frederika and her daughter Christina worsened to the point that Frederika "kicked Christina out of the house." Christina was

110

seventeen years old at the time. When Frederika was a teenager, she had developed a pattern of running away from home. Christina continued the cycle of her mother's relationship with her own parents, estranged from yet inextricably tied to each other. How much the move contributed to the increased tensions between mother and daughter and to the progress of Frederika's disease is a question Frederika's death leaves with us. She again found herself in a foreign environment, isolated from established relationships.

I am grateful to Frederika for giving permission to publish her story. Through her, we are reminded again that the horrors of the past continue to haunt the lives of survivors and their inter- and intrapersonal relationships. I deeply regret not having had an opportunity to meet her.

I didn't want to hear the Nazis were going to march in Skokie. I got so enraged. Everything came back to me, how we were barricaded in our street, identified in every way, on our clothes, on our papers. They came in the neighborhood, those men, they marched and broke everything. My father and mother were held, not like humans, but like animals. The humiliation, that's what bothers me.

I just wished I was powerful; I would take a gun and shut them all up. When I came to this country, I wanted to leave everything behind, but I didn't forget. And it could start all over here. I have avoided talking about the Holocaust. I don't know what is the point, if people who have been hungry even, or poor, can know the meaning of what happened. At one time I wanted to become an American citizen, but [now] I'm so glad I changed my mind. My husband tried to explain to me about rights and freedoms in this country, but you see, the Nazis could come again.

I function, but sometimes I fall apart thinking about it. I cannot cope with anything. I'm back there, a little girl six years old. When I say my house, it's not the house I live in now. I mean my house when I was a kid, my house in Bratislav, Slovakia. Somehow my memory goes very far back. When I was two years old, my father took me on the bicycle. He was turning, and the bicycle slided on the sand, and he fell with me. I remember the fall, the pain. Until I was six and a half, seven, I thought I was happy, really happy. Even though we already had bombing, some trouble in my town, and there was no candy or chocolate, still, I felt happy. When I got out of school each day, I didn't have far to go. I would not go home; I would stay in the street. I would watch the bombs falling on the factories, and when it was over my mother would ask where I was, but I felt I was strong and nothing would happen to me.

When I was five or six years old playing with other kids who were not Jewish, I knew they were not our friends. If we want for a walk in the park, kids would get together and yell at me. Or parents would call their children away from me. Still my father would try to keep me away from them, to keep them from saying something unkind to me.

We celebrated the holidays at home, and I remember as a little girl going to a synagogue, sitting on the balcony. It wasn't like here; men and women didn't mix. My mother would sit and talk with her sisters-in-law. When my father was called to read from the Torah, all my aunts would hang over the balcony, listening. My father was the only boy, the youngest of his family of nine children. You could not even touch him down there, reading. He was God to me.

My mother's family was Hungarian and Austrian all the way back, not Jewish. They were bankers and lived in a house they didn't have funds to keep up. My mother had a title, baroness, but my father had the money. He came along and bought out her family's properties, that's how my parents met. There was a real fight because my mother's family didn't want her to marry a Jewish man, even though it was his money that let them eat. Sometimes my mother seemed more Jewish to me than he did.

My father was arrested by the Germans the first time in Paris in 1939. I don't know if he was there on business, or why, but he escaped. After that we were watched. When he came back home, he began printing papers. There were no jobs, no money. He would go to Vienna to get black market food as part of an organization in our neighborhood. Then my father left again, and my mother cried a lot. I resented that my father was always out doing something.

He started to fall apart. When he heard planes coming or the sirens, or someone knock on the door, my father got pale and green and very scared. I didn't understand. My mother had shiny bright glossy eyes and high cheekbones; she looked like a skeleton, just two bones sticking out. She was always so quiet. Now I understand she was worrying that there was no food, but at that time I didn't realize it because she was always saying, ''Food will come somehow.'' My mother would be scared too, but she would never say it. She had two friends, Dorka and Deborah, who worked in a restaurant. Sometimes she would leave me and go meet them and share leftovers with them from the restaurant. Someone familiar with the city told me about a playhouse where they served food, and I would wait 'til lunchtime or dinnertime was over and go behind the theater to go through the garbage. A dog could have had more than I had then. Maybe if I was just a little older, maybe I could have understood.

There were different people who took over our building while my father was in hiding, printing underground and all of that. Some people moved into my uncle's beautiful apartment, this man from the party and his two kids, just took it over food and all. I thought they were ugly kids. And downstairs from us was a doctor and his wife and small baby. The wife was always putting flowers in the windows, spring flowers in a beautiful hand-painted vase. I was always looking up at the window, and my mother would explain the shape, the forms, show me how it was so special. Then another young couple came to live in their apartment. They made lots of noise, and I don't know what happened to the doctor and his wife and baby who used to live there. After they moved, I was playing in the court, and I saw this new woman take the other lady's hand-painted vase and put her own flowers in it. I felt she had violated something. It hurts me still today how they took over everything, the Nazis.

So in 1942 I had a new home, a neighborhood where everybody was Jewish and everybody had to have authorization to get out to go shopping, and had to wear the star on the back. The Slovaks were very cooperative with the Nazis. They knew what was happening, and they abandoned everybody. We lived in there for a while, but because someone in our family was Catholic, we were able to move out of this area to a different apartment in a tall building on Firsch Avenue. Some kids had a father, and some kids didn't. If you didn't, it was bad. I had a father, so I needed to say that. There was a small courtyard in back of our building; maybe it used to be nice, but it got smelly and dirty. I would talk with the kids and play there, and my mother would listen. She was always listening. Suddenly she would call me inside and tell me I shouldn't say whatever I had just said, and after that I could not go out anymore. At that time my father was hiding behind a wall in the apartment, going out at night, and when I started to tell that to one of the other kids, I got a very bad spanking.

I went to a Catholic school, St. Terezin school. I don't remember learning, just eating, sitting at the table. I was there for first grade, but eventually the sisters closed their door and I was out. We wanted to go anywhere, but no country would take us. Even though my father knew people in the embassy, even though we finally got a passport, but the Germans were already in Bratislav.

My mother went to the *commanditure* and talked to them. She said we had a Christian education, but they said we had to prove it. We went back to the priest at the Catholic school to get a certificate saying I was at that school longer than I really was, but the priest had been shot by that time. The whole convent had been hiding people. My uncle had some communication with the Vatican. Pope Pius at that time signed 6,000 birth certificates, and my uncle was going to try to get them for us. But I came home one day and found my parents gone. It was the first time they had both left me. A man was waiting there in a black leather coat. He sent me away to the country where I stayed with some people who didn't know what to do with me. Then they sent me to Terezin in Moravia. It was a place where they decided where we'd go next. It was summer, and it was hot and there was no water, only two or three times a day we got water by waiting in line. Lots of kids were dying, lots of kids, and I knew it. The trucks were taking everybody out that died each day, but it wasn't so bad as later. Terezin was the beginning for me of learning what could happen to us. I met up with my mother again in Terezin; she had been sent there too.

I got a huge abscess on my groin. My mother was going crazy because I could not walk and she was worried about blood poisoning. Eventually somehow she got some care for me. They had assured her they would give me some anesthesia, but then they took me away and they didn't give me anything; they just took me and put me on the table and held me as they cut through me. The pain was so bad, but I didn't pass out. My mother was there when I was taken back to a room, and I remember passing blood for a long time. My mother got water and boiled it, but there was no antibiotic. I was so angry with my mother for letting them do this to me. I remember it was a very cold winter when it started, my not talking. For six years I never talked again to anybody.

While we were in Terezin, somebody delivered to my mother a false birth certificate signed by the pope with my name on it, saying I was Catholic. Then spring came up, and my mother was taking me outside. Then my mother went away. They said she went to my father. She had been getting cards from him through the Red Cross. I never found out what happened, if my mother found my father or what. That summer I was alone in the camp. Other women took care of me for washing. I had a big scab on top of my head. I didn't see it on me, but I saw it on other people. It was huge, or at least I imagined it was huge and crusty and green, and under it was a nest of lice. It was horrible because some of the lice were so big, but I spent hours watching them. It would be a terrible pain when they were chewing through, and I thought if I scraped off the scab the lice would go away too and there would be nothing left; I would be all alone. It was like I was hiding the lice from somebody, and they were mine. You know, those lice were a comfort to me. It sounds so crazy, but at least something was close to me; I knew them. I had my hair shaved off because of the lice. I had something else, other bugs that made tunnels under the skin. The more I itched, the deeper the wounds would get.

I stayed one summer in Terezin, but winter I was in Houbetin outside of Prague on the German border. They called it a work camp, but I never worked there. On my papers they put down "assumed Slovak" as a nationality.

Before she left, my mother told me I should be sick, to go to the hospital, and I did. I got very sick in Houbetin, with an infection of some kind. I went to this hospital, a children's hospital, and people came to visit me who were friends of my parents. I had seen them together before. Then this German couple came along. I don't know who they were; the man was a German officer, and they had a teenage girl of their own they visited in the hospital. They took me to their home and gave me very good food, but I was very confused, and I was thinking the food was poisoned. Then one night we traveled to Austria where there was some kind of a school with lots of singing and exercising. The German couple left me there, and I didn't see them anymore. The women at the school wore white blouses and the men too. They served lots of raw vegetables and cucumbers and apples. I remember the smell of the food. They measured me, my forehead, my nose and my chin, the separation of my eyes. By that time my hair had grown back, and it was braided. I was the child with the darkest hair there.

Then there was this man; I assume he was a doctor. He stayed with me for hours and talked to me in Russian and Slovak. He had a heavy German accent. I could speak Slovak and Russian too, but I would not speak at all. He did not know which language was mine. But then he spoke to me in French. At my house we had a woman who lived with us and taught me French; she sang to me French songs. When this doctor said to me in French that I would be a donkey, a "baudet," and be put in a corner, I understood him, and I don't know why, but that word, *baudet,* just made me laugh to hear it. Then the doctor took my hand and shook it, and he gave me a red apple. I made designs in it with a knife, so they gave me paper. I prepared the paper by making lines the right height for writing letters, but I made designs instead. Every time I made a house with lots of flowers. There were never people in my pictures.

Lots of people came to examine me. They were very frustrated with me because I wouldn't speak. The women were rough when they got me undressed or washed. They were not nice at all, but it was clean in the hospital and a change from all that dirt in Terezin.

Years later in France, I learned this was the place where they took the Polish children who were good-looking and normal-featured. There were lots of young women from the country who had been sent there to get pregnant with the Nazi officers, I guess, to breed children. Right away when they were born, the babies were taken from them and the women were sent away to a camp, but the children stayed alive. There was a section where you could go to see the babies. Lots of those children must still be living somewhere in Austria or Germany.

After the children's hospital, I was sent with lots of people on a train, and I ended up at Auschwitz. There was dirt, dirt, dirt even under my skin, the dirt. We had to take turns washing. The older people would talk about being gassed while they were in the showers, wondering if they'd be killed this time, and when the kids my age came back from washing, they would say they had been gassed and they were still alive, but it was a disinfectant they went through. I was thinking if I go through this washing, I'm going to die, so I learned to hide under the barracks when it was my turn to take a shower. They had holes outside to go to the bathroom; you had to stand on planks while you were going. But I stopped doing that, too, outside because some people would fall into the holes. People used the barracks when they had to go to the bathroom instead because they were too sick to go out, or too scared. The stink was terrible, and almost everybody got sick with cholera or typhoid. They didn't give us food. Whatever food came, somebody would force you to give up.

I don't remember being shaved again, but I didn't have any hair left when they liberated Auschwitz. I didn't walk; I had abscesses on my feet. They took me to the Red Cross for those abscesses. They put sulphur cream all over me for the parasites under my skin. It was like a thick grease that wouldn't wash off. It took a long time for those parasites to go away.

The people at the Red Cross assumed I was French because I seemed to respond most to French, of all the languages they tried, so the Red Cross gave me to the French Red Cross and I went to Strasbourg. It was spring in France in 1946; birds were chirping. I didn't walk, I was skin and bones, diseased, awful. My mother always told me the Red Cross was safe, but they were giving me lots of shots there. They would examine me, stick things in my throat. I didn't realize they were helping me; it felt like a continuation of whatever happened to me before. I didn't know the war was over. I still heard popping from the mines; the trains were still going by. I screamed all the time. I would hang onto people and my bed, not to be taken away, even to go to the table to eat. Eventually they brought food to me in bed. I think I could have fed myself, but I wanted to be fed.

The food looked terrible, and I thought they were going to poison me. But there was a French doctor and his wife who assisted him and took care of the children. They came to take care of me. They took some bites first from the spoon, and I would see it going down all right, and then I would eat it myself. Slowly I started talking to this doctor. One day he said he was going to be taking all the children somewhere in big buses, and I got very panicky, hysterical. He and his wife decided to take me out of the hospital to stay with them. They never really got papers made, but they wanted to adopt me.

Frederika

When I was thirteen, the Red Cross reunited me with my parents, but I didn't want to go with them. There was a big fight because the doctor and his wife wanted to keep me, and my parents said I was to be with them. My parents won. You know that choking pain I get? That was the first time when I had a tightening in my chest. My father used to be a nice man, a fun man, a good-looking man. After he came back, he was still good-looking, but he changed. He didn't smile anymore. He had this anger under him, and he didn't talk. He used to explain things to me; now he was very harsh. He looked like a living death, his eyes were so deep and so far, so empty, he didn't have eyes anymore. I felt I was so so close he hated me, or so far away I didn't exist. My mother in between us would cling to my father. I think she would have let me go, back to the doctor, just away. If she had a choice between me and my father, she'd choose my father always. Sometimes my father would punish me. I assume he felt very guilty for having brought me into the world. I remembered as a little girl how scared he was, how he could not protect me. Three or four times when I was fourteen or fifteen I threw this in his face. I would tell him "I was on my own for seven years, now you try to do everything for me, in a way. Where were you when all this happened?" Then my mother would be angry with me. "You have no right to judge anyone. You should have respect for your parents."

After the war in France, there was no food, no clothes, but I was too young to understand why we still had to have a ration card, why there wasn't enough bread. And on top of that my parents decided on a new life. Now they wanted me to erase my religion. Suddenly we were to be like everybody around us. Sunday everybody would go to church. My mother said, "You go for all of us. You're our representative."

It was hard, the coping. I was tall, like I am now, but very skinny. I was sick. My brain functioned; that was the strangest part. I was always ahead of the kids my age intellectually, but not physically and not emotionally. Part of me was missing even then. I hear now the Vietnam veterans who came back, they get help, but there wasn't that kind of help then at all.

The kids I met at school were very different from me. They didn't know anything about us. I had to hide the fact that we were Jewish. One time we went on some kind of a field trip. We went down into some army tanks and over holes in the ground, like from bombs. The children asked me where I had been during the war, and I ran away. I just wandered in the country and slept in a barn for two or three days. My parents could not find me. After that, I ran away often. My mother was very uptight about me washing and keeping clean. It was crazy to me after all those years I didn't wash. I would go to this French family. They never asked any questions. They let me use one room, and if I wanted to eat, it was fine; if I didn't want to, that was fine too.

We really did not have a country anymore. Nobody wanted us. I don't know why. My father went to England to try to get us into the United States, but there was no way. He said it was because of the Rosenberg trial. He wanted also to go to Israel and farm. He even learned about growing pineapples and oranges; we had books, books, books about farming. His dream was having oranges all over everywhere. Of course, we never made it to Israel. We got all the way to Switzerland, and we had to come back. We were always going somewhere, anywhere.

We ended up in Sydney, Australia. My father had a job on a sheep farm. It was out in the middle of nowhere and took the truck forever to get there. To me it was fun. You could run all over. I was not sleeping with my parents, in the same building; they were sleeping somewhere else. But then at meal time we ate in one big room, the adults at one table, the kids at another. My father enjoyed it too in Australia, but my mother wasn't too healthy. She couldn't take the heat. It was a rough country, and there were many fights. She wanted me to get out. Me, I never was sick the whole eighteen months we lived in Australia.

We came back to France for a while and lived with friends. My father got a job in a factory as a chemist working with dyes. He did very well working for those people. Eventually we owned a little farm and a small apartment in southern France. Every Saturday I had to cut fresh flowers from our home and take them to the priest at church. I was a teenager then, and to tell you the truth, he was not much of a priest.

It was not bad those years in France, except there was no happiness in our family. I met people, Polish people, who went through the war and had children. They had fun; I heard laughing. But with my parents, it was the end. My father always made me feel that my body would go on, but I was dead. I felt for many years that I had nothing left inside. Ten years later, we went back to Germany to visit. My father wanted to thank the people who were hiding him during the war. They helped him escape and all, but when we went back there, they held this feeling of superiority over us. I wanted to see the people being sad and sorry, ashamed. But they weren't. They were glad; they were smiling.

I went to visit my aunt in Budapest for two days in 1957. I saw pictures from the old days. She was going to send them with me, but I never had a chance. The war came in Budapest; lots of people died fighting while I was stuck there. My aunt was so worried something would happen to me. We went for a walk and that was it; she crossed me to the Danube, to the American embassy. From there I went to Vienna. I never had time to say good-bye.

When I was a teenager, I just wanted to escape all the reminders of those days I was not a person. I wasn't treated as a person. I was dating German men, always hiding it that I was Jewish. But eventually they would find out. I went to boarding school and all the girls I knew, by the time they were twenty-one, they were getting married. Everybody treated me like I was old enough, but I wasn't ready. Many years I felt I did not want my parents. Sometimes I would meet adopted people, grown-ups who said they would want to know who they were. I said, My God! They don't know nothing about themselves. They could take right then that moment and just be born. They search back, they dig. I didn't want this.

When I was twenty-eight, a friend called and invited me to go to an American football game. I had never been to one before. It was a demonstration game the American army was playing. There was a party after the game, and I went. My [future] husband was alone in a corner, and I felt sorry for him so I went over to talk. He was born in Germany and had only lived in the United States six years. He started college there, but that was a burden to his family, so he joined the army in the special services and requested to go to Europe. He was good-looking, and he had this crewcut. I thought he looked like President Kennedy. I felt if I ever marry someone, it will be someone like Kennedy. Besides, I wanted to go to the United States and get away from my parents, so I married him.

My father-in-law has a very strong German accent. It's rough, cruel, sharp. A person with a German accent could be the nicest person, but I cannot deal with a German accent. It puts me back there; it reminds me. Last year when I went to Florida, someone broke in and took all of our things. It gave me a crazy feeling, like being raped, the way I felt when everything was taken away from us in Slovakia when someone took over my doll, my clothes. I can't stand for anyone to touch my things now without my permission, or that feeling comes back. My father-in-law was a Nazi. I saw him in his black uniform in the family photo albums. My mother-in-law had a khaki uniform worn by a woman active in the party, a uniform like a girl scout's. She said once her father was in Auschwitz, poor man, working there as a conductor on a railroad. One time a documentary was on when she was at our place. They showed a man on a train coming out of Czechoslovakia. I said maybe that's where your father was working. She blushed and didn't answer.

Those first years we were married were not productive. My husband had this mental hangup and couldn't work. Because of our financial situation, every winter I got thrown back to those times in my childhood when there was no work, no money. In Austria there was still property in my mother's name. My mother's brothers and sisters were still living in her family's house, but the American government wanted to buy all of that land to put a base with missiles on it. In Austria you have to pay taxes on property, or if you don't, in twenty-one years you lose it. For all that time, no one had ever paid the taxes, so eventually my mother would lose the house if she didn't agree to sell. She refused to sign the papers. Her sister, who was married to a German and living in Israel, found out about the Americans wanting to buy the property. She said she would pay for everything if my mother would just sign. But my mother wouldn't listen to my aunt. For many years there had been a family dispute, everybody blaming everybody for their troubles. They all blamed my mother for marrying a Jewish man, and she was angry at them because they had been happy to take his money when they needed it to eat.

My aunt came to see me to ask me if I would talk to my mother about selling the house, so I went to see her. My mother said, "The property was in the family for a very long time. Pabla wants me to sign those papers because she wants more money. We didn't have it before, and we won't have it now. I'm not signing." My husband said if she didn't want the money for herself, she should take it for her daughter. We had only been married a few months, and we could have used it. Then my mother jumped on my husband. She said he had nothing to do with it; he wasn't going to tell her what to do. He married me, and he should take care of me.

Then our first baby, Christina, was born. Three years later, I got pregnant again. I felt the baby was pressuring, blocking something. I had the feeling of icy water running up and down, or of scraping paste, liquid sandpaper going down my leg. I felt even my skin changed in color. My doctor said he didn't see nothing and sent me to another doctor. He said, "It's all in your head," and that was the end of it.

For six years I complained to my doctor about my feeling in my leg. I felt I had wax on my face. I could not open my hand completely; it was stiff, and when I would move, the skin would split. I had cramps around my intestines and lots of headaches. They put me in the hospital. Then everybody was explaining I have calcium in my artery; it's getting clogged up. I have scleroderma. They explained my body was hardening, the motility was going out. The more they explained, the more sick I got. I felt pain all in my arm. I was worried falling asleep, I felt that tightening.

By this time, our daughter Christina was six years old. I said I didn't want to go to church anymore myself, but I figured I should have our daughter baptized to please my husband. Her first year, she went to a public school, but then my husband said Catholic schools are better. I visited St. Clara School, and the next year Christina went there. I really tried. I participated in everything the school had. I even prayed like a Catholic, though I still didn't understand the religion. I went to the church often, not every Sunday, but to Communion and all of that. But I never told my husband that I resented it, that I was giving away something of me to the wrong thing. I looked at Christina and her blue eyes, little nose, long hair, and I said yes, she belongs there. But not me.

After our son, Barry, came, I got very uptight about this Catholic business. In our family in Slovakia, for a boy it was very important, our religion, to study and everything. My boy cousins were always super. Girls learn how to cook, how to clean house. But boys! It must be all the way. They are smart. I waited, but I could not have Barry baptized. I told my mother-in-law to go for me to church or to school for me, and I would write a note saying I couldn't go. Finally, I decided I was never going back.

I didn't like Christina coming home from school very upset, crying, feeling very pious about everything. That bothered me. She was talking about being a nun. During the war, a young girl who was Jewish married a Christian, and her husband actually sold out her whole family. Their daughter, who looks Jewish and is Jewish, she's a nun.

Christina felt so uptight about herself, reading in the library about St. Agnes and Bernadette from Lourdes, all those who were canonized, and she'd come up with these questions. I could not follow her. I didn't have any answers for her. I didn't have any answers for myself because I don't know so much about Judaism, except what I saw in my family before the war. To tell you the truth, the Catholic religion to me was barbaric by then. Christina was getting to the point where God was talking to her; an angel was flying on top of her. When she came home and didn't want to wash, I didn't know why. A substitute teacher told her if she washed and touched her intimate parts, she would make a sin. She was so upset she had committed a sin so many times before, she had to go to confession. But little girls had only two, three times a year when they could go to confession. In the meantime, she was wearing all those medals and crosses the teacher had given her, and she wouldn't take them off. I didn't know about the substitute teacher at that time. I said, "Take those off, Christina, those plastic beads and strings, they're smelly. Why are you wearing them?"

She said, "I have to because I committed lots of sins." This substitute teacher had told her the devil was in our house. Christina said that was why I was sick. Then she was more upset than before. I called Sister Judy and mentioned this man's name. She said, "Oh, he's a fanatic." But still this man goes to the hospital to visit sick people. He brings them crosses and all. The priest knows it and doesn't do anything about it. I talked to the priest once, too, and he said that man was a very religious man, maybe a little obnoxious with his faith, but not a mean man. Maybe he isn't physically mean, but in other ways he is. After that, Christina went to public school.

Probably I'm a terrible mother. I look at my kids itching from a dry scalp and think maybe they got something. I was upset about this, and at their school I would ask, but the teachers always say no, they didn't discover anything. It was horrible. I went through their heads myself, but my husband said, "You're crazy. In this country we don't have lice." I said, "Yes, we do. I heard sometimes in schools they do." Barry would say to me, "What are you looking for, Mom?" And I said for little bugs. That worried him.

I'm very uptight about food. I don't allow Bernard or Christina to leave the table without cleaning their plates. I don't push on them food they don't like, and I let them take as much as they want, but they have to eat it all. I would like them to know how valuable food is. My husband cleans his plate; he eats everything. It's one of the things I did like about him from the beginning. He always says thank you for his food, for making it. When my son comes home with half a sandwich uneaten, I put it in the refrigerator, or I would eat it, or my daughter would say, "Okay, I'll eat it." I know it's unappetizing to her, but she eats it anyway because she knows it hurts me to waste food at all. But then I feel guilty for making her eat the leftovers, and I make her a milkshake or give her chocolates. I go crazy when we go to a restaurant and see waiters carrying away food on people's plates. I feel like hitting them. I want to stand up and insult the people. "If you don't want to eat it, don't order it." The Germans were very spoiled, just like that.

A few days ago, someone hit us when we were driving our car, made a big dent and a hole. The lady knew she did it; she looked back at us then, zoom, she drove away. I said to my husband, "I have the license number. Let's go to the police." My husband didn't want to go. I said, "You have three hundred dollars' damage to the car, and I have the license number of the person who did it, so we're going to go." We spent an hour at the police station. We found the woman, and while I was sitting in the car, she gave my husband all the information for the insurance company, and she said she didn't realize she hit us so hard. She apologized, and my husband told her to forget it because she was being so nice. When he told me this, I said, "How could you?" He said they were going to have problems with their insurance if we reported it. I said, "Who gives a damn? Believe me, if I did that, they'd be after me. We're not going to cheat her; we're going to let the insurance company pay for it." He was upset, and I was too because it was 7:30 and that TV program on the Holocaust was starting at 8:00, and I wanted to get home to see it.

Frederika

I didn't want to watch this Holocaust movie with my husband. I didn't want to hear his comments. I thought maybe he'd say something nasty, or maybe he'd feel sorry for me. I didn't want him to feel sorry; I just wanted to go away and stay away for a while. I thought I was going to fall apart after the picture, but it was not as painful as I thought it would be because they did not show any of the bodies of the prisoners, the lice, the cholera. It was all gray and green in the camps, but in the movie everything was nice pretty colors, people were lying there quiet, the way they showed on TV. But there was not one minute, day or night, when there was quiet in the camps. Always somebody had pain. They didn't show this, or the cold, so freezing cold, or the smell, inside, outside. In the middle of a garbage dump, I close my eyes and say it doesn't stink as bad as where I was; it's nothing to compare. So they told the story, but still nobody will know.

My husband watched the program with me. It really stirred him up. He walked away, he came back, he got angry at me and at Christina because we wanted to watch it. Christina asked quite a few times about Hitler and about Grandpa in Germany. He said he wasn't too sure about Grandpa because he was always traveling back and forth, and Grandma was in Czechoslovakia. Then he said, ''No wonder Hitler wanted to do away with you Jews. You have tough blood.'' I got very hurt. It was the way he said it. He had always made me feel good about myself, really good. I thought he liked me being smart, but this time he turned it against me. I was so angry, I said, ''If you feel so guilty about your family and are so aware of paying everything back, you can go to Israel and work in a kibbutz for a year. Work on a farm over there; carry a gun. You don't make any money here, anyway. Maybe after that you'll be less uptight about being married to me.'' He looked at me and said, ''Yeah, at least my life would have a purpose.'' We'd never talked about this before. That night my husband was out until about two o'clock in the morning, and I didn't say anything about it. His clothes smelled like smoke from the taverns.

After the Holocaust special, Christina got a rash on her neck, and her skin on her arm began to crack. But I felt pretty good. The swelling in my feet has gone down some. This winter I coped maybe a little better. But even if something would happen and my husband would earn enough so we could buy a small place of our own, it still would not feel like it's mine. I'd still be missing something.

Sometimes I look at Christina and notice she is starting to get a rounded behind. She's growing up so fast. I see in her something I couldn't have myself when I was growing up. I would wish it on myself, her life. I'm happy because she's having it all. She's going to be a very pretty girl, but sometimes I worry she's just going to be a dumb girl. She could have good report cards from school, but she gets bad ones sometimes, and I think she throws it all away, everything she has, and she could just end up working somewhere in a factory or someplace like that.

I saw my parents six or seven years ago. My father looks young, holds himself straight and keeps himself neat, old-fashioned looking. My mother, too. She never wears makeup. She gets up at three in the morning, and her chignon is up, neat. She's never slouchy. I never saw her messy. My father is not nice to my mother. Even today—he is sixty-six, and my mother is sixty-two—she's his slave, completely devoted to him. If my father would die, my mother would not survive.

I like to keep in touch with my parents now. For a long time, I didn't know where they were. They're living all alone on top of a mountain in southern France. They have a spa, because my father collected damages from the war, and the treatments are all paid for by social security. They write to me in Slovak. I asked my mother where I could get my birth certificate. She wrote back that I was delivered by a midwife, the birth certificate was done in a court, and there were two witnesses certifying everything, but the place where I was born doesn't exist anymore. She said maybe in the Vatican is a copy of the birth certificate signed by the pope, but that would be it. The only papers about me start after the war in France. I asked her where I was in school. She answered that the school in Bratislav was destroyed, and the synagogue was probably closed down too. It upset me a little bit. Then she asked me how I was, how my husband was doing. She asked more about the kids than she ever did before. My father didn't write at all this time. I guess I hurt him by asking questions, reminding him. He's probably doing fine.

I understand my parents, but I understand without talking with them because they still do not want to talk to me. They feel guilty that they didn't get away or kill themselves and me when the Holocaust happened. My husband says I find excuses for them. It's not excuses; I try to take their place. My two kids help me to be my father, to be my mother, to have their feelings.

I think my mother was torn apart by her family and her husband. She was always presented with making a choice between them. I think I picked my husband because he's so far apart from my father. Everything my father is, my husband is not. I have a little something about men. I feel man uses women; even today women are so dependent on men. Even as a little girl I felt that way. I rebelled. A man to me is almost an enemy, a challenge. When I see a man, in every way I'm very careful. My father controlled me completely as a teenager until I got out from home at twenty-two. I could not take my husband controlling money, telling me what to spend. I could not take a man who would do that to me. I'm not a money spender. I'm a planner, and my husband is impulsive. I think he likes me this way, but he throws it at me many times. When I'm angry, I think I should have married someone else like my parents wanted me to marry.

I miss family. I have beautiful memories of my childhood vacations, holidays, food, cooking together. I was the youngest child in this whole bunch of relatives. There were séances [*sic*] of taking pictures when the family was together. I was always up front or held up high. My old, old, old, grandparents, my aunt who was ninety and some, had stories to tell. She made terrible cookies; they tasted like everything and nothing all at once. She was old-fashioned and delicate in her long black skirt, but she was independent, living alone. She was like a tradition. Uraniny, we called her. Uraniny is coming. My daughter never will have that. After I grew up, I never had it anymore myself.

Yesterday was Mother's Day. I hate the Italians, my neighbors. God, they had cousins, kissing and hugging; they kept coming all afternoon with food. All the mothers had corsages. Here I was alone. I had nobody to kiss, to welcome. I'm not profoundly happy; I didn't find the place I wanted to be. I have this pain in my heart, some strange feeling. Whatever I want I will never have. Some people feel satisfied; they have achieved things. They have two cars, a beautiful patio, they are good-looking people, healthy. Something inside me is never going to be filled up, no matter what I have. I would like to give my kids something I'll never be able to give.

Even today I feel this is not my country, this is not where I belong, though I don't carry my passport anymore, my papers. Many years I had everything ready to go. Now I only have my driver's license. But spiritually I don't think I have found myself. I still have that pinch here over my heart.

When I began to have my first problems with my kidneys, my doctor said one was all choked up with calcium and was on the blink. He said, "Don't worry, we can find a donor. Nowadays the operation could be successful." The more he talked about what was wrong, the more I made it happen, the sicker I got. Last spring when I was in the hospital, they could not put any needles in me because my skin, all of me, was hard. I said, "What's the use? I'm calcifying all over." After the last time when I was in the hospital, they put me on a computer that goes from all Northwestern hospital patients, and they follow me.

But I eat very well these days; I haven't had any choking lately. The doctor said I would have to have dilation a couple times a week, but now he is surprised because my throat is more open. I haven't had to go to him in many months. I didn't have to have my teeth removed the way he thought. I have more friends. Before, when it was cold, I felt a tightening on my face, like wax. When I have this feeling now, when my hand is stiff,

I don't think of the skin splitting; I think of stretching, smoothing. I used to have lots of cramps around my intestines. I always imagined calcium taking over, and the whole thing is going to harden up. If I get a cramp now, I think of relaxing, and I pour someting warm inside me. If I have to have a test, I relax and go soft, and I have no problem. I had lots of headaches before. Now, instead of saying I have this hot iron squashing me, if I feel tension, I say oh well, and I shake my head and try to loosen up the skin and push blood into it. Instead of just thinking that's it, I'm turning to stone. I can think about it and make it go the other way.

I think if I had listened to myself with all my problems inside myself and not the lamentations of the other people who knew me saying, "My God, poor Zadenka, I feel so sorry for you," I would have been a lot better off. The way they said, "How are you?" the way I heard that tone of voice, I thought, "Oh, I feel terrible." I think, yes, you can get yourself to feel miserable. Especially yesterday, Mother's Day, just sitting in a restaurant, my husband grumbling, I felt like walking out of that place. I said, "Please, if you don't smile in one minute . . ." Positive thinking is a big help.

I use the Carl Simington relaxing tape, and it's fantastic. I close my eyes, and I always see I'm back in my country. I see the butter factory in Bratislav, and a big carnival my parents always took me to, and a playhouse where students played. On Thursday there was a program on the radio, and I can hear that smooth beautiful voice, like music, telling fairy tales. "Hello, this is Hela." I see the butterflies, everything smelling nice, my family at a picnic. I stop it, and I stay there. I imagine the sun shining on my face, melting the cold away.

Bibliography

Kestenberg, Judith. *Newsletter of the Jerome Ryker International Study of Organized Persecution of Children* (Sands Point, N.Y.), Summer 1985.

Kestenberg, Judith S., and Ira Brenner. "Children Who Survived the Holocaust: Role of Rules and Routines in Development of the Superego." *International Journal of Psycho-analysis* 67 (1986): 309–316.

Kestenberg, Milton. "Legal Aspects of Child Persecution During the Holocaust." *Journal of Child Psychiatry* 24, no. 4 (July 1985): 381–384.

Krell, Robert. "Child Survivors: 40 Years Later." *Journal of Child Psychiatry* 24, no. 4 (July 1985): 397–400.

Miller, Alice. *For Your Own Good.* New York: Farrar, Strauss, Giroux, 1987.

Mosse, George. *Nazi Culture.* New York: Schocken Books, 1951.

Moscovitz, Sarah. *Love Despite Hate.* New York: Schocken Books, 1983.

Pines, Dinna. "Working with Women Survivors of the Holocaust: Affective Experiences in Transference and Countertransference." *International Journal of Psycho-analysis* 67 (1986): 295–306.

Rothenberg, Mira. *Children with Emerald Eyes.* New York: Pocket Books, 1977.

Vegh, Claudine. *I Didn't Say Goodbye.* New York: Dutton, 1979.

Julie Heifetz is Writer-in-Residence for the Center for Holocuast Studies in St. Louis. She has performed her first-person narrative poems based on her interviews with witnesses to the Holocaust throughout the United States. She received her B.A. in English and psychology and her M.A. in psychiatric counseling and education from St. Louis University. She has participated in poetry workshops at Rochester University and Washington University. She was in private practice in psychotherapy for parents of young children, and was co-founder and associate director of the Child Development Project of the St. Louis Psychoanalytic Institute. Her poems have appeared in River Styx, Pax, *and* The Reconstructionist, *and the anthologies* Blood to Remember: An Anthology of American Poets on the Holocaust *and* An Anthology of Missouri Women Poets. *She has written the libretto to the oratorio* Sparrow's Song *as well as a short musical theater piece,* Jenny's Place. *Her previous books are* Gordie's Present *and* Oral History and the Holocaust.

The manuscript was prepared for publication by Christina Postema. The typeface for the text is Times Roman and the display is Mistral and Times Roman. The book is printed on 55-lb. Glatfilter text paper and bound in Holliston Mills Roxite Linen. Manufactured in the United States of America.